THE BOOK OF RIGHT
CHANGE, JEONG YEOK
正易

THE BOOK OF RIGHT CHANGE, JEONG YEOK

正易

A New Philosophy of Asia

Written by Kim Hang

Translated by Sung Jang Chung

iUniverse, Inc.
New York   Bloomington

The Book of Right Change, Jeong Yeok 正易
A New Philosophy of Asia

iUniverse books may be ordered through booksellers or by contacting:

iUniverse
1663 Liberty Drive
Bloomington, IN 47403
www.iuniverse.com
1-800-Authors (1-800-288-4677)

ISBN: 978-1-4502-1082-9 (pbk)
ISBN: 978-1-4502-1083-6 (ebook)

Printed in the United States of America

iUniverse rev. date: 5/20/2010

CONTENTS

ILLUSTRATIONS

ACKNOWLEDGMENTS

I humbly express my deepest gratitude to Gautama Buddha, Maitreya Buddha, Jesus, Confucius, Kim Hang, and Paramahansa Yogananda for their supernal teachings that have been showing me the path of self-realization. I would like to acknowledge those authors cited in the References of this book for their intellectual help, support and validation of my work as well as those authors not cited in the References for their knowledge through my readings contributing to development of the theories, commentaries, and translations written in this book.

I am very thankful to Dr. Chong Chul Yook for his life-long encouragement in our study of *the Jeong Yeok*, and his valuable review of my manuscript related to *the Jeong Yeok*. I would like to specially express my sincere gratitude to the late Dr. Jeong Ho Yi for his teachings in his outstanding books on the subjects of *the Jeong Yeok* and *the I Ching* which he sent me personally after their publications in Korea and decades-long encouragement in my studying of *the Jeong Yeok* and *the I Ching*. I am also thankful to the late Kyung Woon Kim for his personal lectures on *the Jeong Yeok* and *the I Ching* that I received at my young age in Korea.

I am pleased to acknowledge the publishers' granting of permissions to quote or copy figures of their authors' books, particularly grateful to Sarah McKechnie, President of the Lucis Trust of the Lucis Publishing Company, and Eunjin Kim, President of the Asian Culture Press in Seoul, Korea.

I would like to specially express my deep and sincere thanks to my wife, Kwang Jun Lee, MD, for her more than five decades-long help in my work in our up and down lives together, and her unsurpassed patience and love.

INTRODUCTION

1. Kim Hang's Life

Kim Hang was a Korean philosopher and a saint (1826-1898). He published his book, 正易 (*Jeong Yeok*, translated as Book of Right Change) in 1885 (Jeong Ho Yi, 정역 [7]).

Kim Hang was born in a quiet village named Dangol on the side of Innae River, Yeon San, Choong Chung-do, in Korea in 1826. His given name was Hang (恒) and his surname Kim (金). Il Bu (一夫, "One Man") was a name called by Confucius in his vision when he was enlightened at his age of 54 years. He was the eldest son of Kim In Ro. He was a descendant of the thirty-seventh king of *Silla* (新羅) dynasty. The "four pillars (四柱)" of his birth: year, month, day and time, are *Byung Sool* (丙戌), *Ki Hae* (己亥), *Byung Ja* (丙子), and *Ki Hae* (己亥).

He was outstandingly bright and wise since his childhood. He loved to study Chinese ancient classic books including Book of Propriety, Book of Poetry, Book of Songs, and Studies of *Seong Ri* (性理, human nature and principle).

At the age of 36 yars (1861), Kim Hang's teacher, Yi Yeon Dam (李蓮潭) told him and said-

1

"You will inherit declining Confucianism and support heaven's time. Isn't it a great thing? Until now I have called you as my disciple but from now on I am going to treat you as my fellow. I am asking you not to study merely the Book of Poetry, the Book of Proprietry or the Book of Ceremony. You would be better off much concentrating in reading *the I Ching* and the Book of History. While so studying, you will advance with your inner perceptive nature and achieve a great deal. You are going to certainly write a book in the future. Please include a stanza of my poem in it."

He gave to Kim Hang a stanza of his poem; it said-

"In viewing clearness, nothing is clearer than water (author's note: water means *kye hae* water, 癸亥水). Loving virtue, one should do *in* (仁, re'n, love-benevolence). The shadow, image of the moon moves at the site of heaven's center moon (author's note: heaven's center moon is thought to be the moon being in conjunction with the sun). I would like to advise you to seek this truth, searching the movement of the moon's shadow."

Yeon Dam gave this cordial request to Kim Hang; thereafter he left Tiwool village aimlessly and whereabouts he went was unknown.

Kim Hang devoted all his efforts to his studies of *the I Ching* and the Book of History, following the cordial request of his teacher, Yeon Dam in order to search the movement of the moon's shadow. He did reasoning and meditation. He overcame all adverse circumstances with patience. In his meditation, he spontaneously recited and sang five vowel sounds: *goong* (宮, "aum"), *sang* (商, "a"), *kak* (角, "ə:"), *chi* (徵, "i:"), and *oo* (羽, "u:") or two vowel sounds:*goong* (宮, "aum") and *sang* (商, "a:"). When advancing in deep meditation and an ecstatic state, he moved his hands and feet, and danced on the ground. His disciples called the kind of meditation with reciting, singing and dancing, "*yeongga- moodo* (詠歌舞蹈)". He did *"yeongga-moodo"* day and night. He came home with his dew-wet clothes in dawn. There was no grass on the spot of the ground where he trodded and danced in the mountain behind Dangol village away from people. According to legends transmitted by his disciples who saw their teacher doing "*yeongga-moodo*", he looked like a holy hermit playing a flute and a white crane flying in the sky.

At the age of fifty-four years, a mysterious eight trigrams began to appear in front of the eyes of Kim Hang and became gradually brighter and filled heaven and earth; it continued to be visible regardless with open or closed eyes for three years. Kim Hang repeatedly read and concentrated all of his efforts on research of *the I Ching* in order to find an explanatory answer to the eight trigrams in his vision that was unknown to *I Ching* scholars.

He eventually found a special description by Confucius in the Discussion of Trigrams (設卦傳, Shuo Kua) in *the I Ching* that exactly matched and described the arrangement of the eight trigrams seen in his vision (*The I Ching*, translated by Richard Willhelm, rendered into English by Cary F Baynes [21]). Kim Hang made Kim Kook Hyun (金國鉉), his nephew and one of his disciples draw the trigrams in the vision.

At this time, unexpectedly, Confucius appeared in his vision of Kim Hang and said-

"At midnight of *ki* and *kap*, *kye hae* (癸亥) is born." Confucius called Kim Hang "Il Bu" (translated "One Man"), and continued to say- "You have accomplished what I intended but did not finish. It is a great thing!"

Confucius congratulated Kim Hang and asked him to do more research.

The eight trigrams observed in Kim Hang's vision continued to be seen for further three more years and finally disappeared.

In this way, the third and new *Jeong Yeok* (正易) Eight Trigrams was drawn. The first *Bok Hui* (伏羲) and the second *Mun Wang* (文王) Eight Trigrams are explicitly described by Confucius in *the I Ching* [21]. Kim Hang was the first scholar in the history of *the I Ching* who discovered that Confucius knew the coming third *Jeong Yeok* and described it in his commentaries to *the I Ching*.

Kim Hang wrote in his book that Confucius is indeed our great teacher for ten thousand generations, and admired Confucius. Confucius' way is "confidence without words' (不言而信) (Richard Wilhelm, *the I Ching* [21]). Confucius knew with confidence and wrote it in his commentaries to *the I Ching* but did not say it publicly.

The above important and extraordinary story regarding the origin of the *Jeong Yeok* (正易) was clarified by a disciple named Kim Hong Hyun (金洪鉉) who was a nephew and one of the most devoted disciples of Kim Hang. He maintained a straw-hatched small house between the "Turtle Rock" and the "Dragon Rock" at the Kooksa Peak of Mount Kyeryong. His residence was used for his teacher and disciples to teach and study. He took care of Teacher, Kim Il Bu and his disciples with his expenses. His disciples and other scholars in surrounding regions called him "a virtuous senior" (Duk Dang, 德堂) and respected him.

When Kim Hang was old and weak, Kim Hong Hyun carried him on his back on mountain roads. One day of the Autumn Holiday (秋夕) in Korea three months prior to Kim Hang's death, while resting on a road where was quiet and away from other people, Kim Hong Hyun politely asked his teacher a question of how his teacher obtained the mysterious *Jeong Yeok* Eight Trigrams. The disciple asked the same question, as a matter of fact, a few years previously but his teacher declined to answer to the disciple's special question. So Kim Hong Hyun was worried that his teacher might scold him for his repeated question. However, this time, Kim Hang unexpectedly said-

"Well, you want so eagerly to know about the origin of the *Jeong Yeok* Eight trigrams, I am going to tell you today."

Kim Hang gave a clear detailed answer to the disciple's sincere question as above described in the preceding page.

This unusual utmost important true story concerning the birth of the *Jeong Yeok* Eight Trigrams was luckily transmitted by Kim Hong Hyun to other disciples including Jeong Ho Yi who published in his books later [8, 23].

I went to Mount Kyeryong when I was young in Korea. I had a fortunate opportunity to meet Kim Hong Hyun who was only one surviving disciple who had studied under Kim Il Bu.

Kim Hang drew *the Jeong Yeok* Eight Trigrams and published *the Jeong Yeok*, the Book of Right Change at the age of 60 yeears in 1885. He said in his book that he wrote what heaven dictated to him. He mastered Confucianism, Buddhism, and Taoism. He foresaw the new world and the new age to come; he wrote in *the Jeong Yeok*, a year of 360 days, a long spring throughout a year without seasons, a right calendar of ten thousand generations without using leap years, emergence of Maitreya Buddha, presence of the creator Father on Earth as in heaven, and boundless goodness in the coming later heaven.

With completion of *the Jeong Yeok,* Kim Hang could successfully answered the cordial request to search the movement of the moon's shadow given him by his teacher, Yeon Dam decades previously. He restored a kind of meditation for cultivating human inner, divine nature and enlightenment that had been discontinued since King Wen for three thousand years: the way of meditation with song and dance; it has been called by his disciples "*yeongga-moodo*" (詠歌舞蹈, recite, sing, and dance).

One day before his death, on the Twenty-fourth Day of November, 1896, year of *Moo Sool* (戊戌), Kim Hang left his last words to his

5

family. He gave a sealed piece of paper to a disciple named Lo Bong Jeong and told him to open it when he would get home at Gong Ju. Kim Hang then made all of his disciples return to their homes. A group of Lo left Dangol on that day and arrived at a village named Lo Seong in the evening on their way home. Lo was so curious and could not help open the piece of paper. When he opened, he found unexpectedly eight Chinese characters of *Moo Sool* (戊戌), *Kap Ja* (甲子), *Kap Sool* (甲戌), and *Moo Jeen* (戊辰). He wondered that the writing might indicate the "four pillars" of his teacher's death: year, month, day and time. The group gave up returning home and left Lo Seong early morning back for Dangol. When they got back to Dangol, their teacher had already passed away; they went into mourning for their teacher. The actual "four pillars" of death of their teacher were literally similar to the writing written in the piece of paper.

Kim Hang died on the Twenty-Fifth Day of November, 1898 (year of *Moo Sool*, month of *Kap Ja*, Day of *Kap Sool*, and Time of *Moo Jeen*, in the morning) at the age of seventy two years. Kim Hang is believed to have known the time of his impending death ahead.

I would like to write about two episodes of predictions made by Kim Hang as by-talks. When he and one of his disciples were once passing between Hyang Han Ri and Kwang Suk villages south of Kooksa Peak (國師峯). Kim Hang pointed with a rod to a spot at the foot of a mountain and told to his disciple and said-

"There will be a hole through here in the mountain that will be for a long metal-fire way (author's note: a metal-fire way 金火道 means a train) passing through." Decades later the Kwang Suk Tunnel was constructed at the same location for a train running the railway.

He predicted a today's airplane to appear in Korea in the future; he named it a "wind-wheel vehicle 風輪車". He talked about the shape and speed of future train and airplane. He thus foretold future transportation machinery of civilization to come to Korea.

I carried with me a copy of *the Jeong Yeok* during the two-month period of my stay in North Korea, where I had been forcefully transported at an early stage of the Korean War in 1950. My belief and faith in the *Jeong Yeok* gave me strength, courage, and guidance (see author's book *Seeking a New World*).

I would like to describe humbly what I have learned and understand myself from my study of the *Jeong Yeok*, carefully avoiding any misunderstanding, prejudice or dogmatism. The purpose of my translating *the Jeoung Yeok* 正易 is to help, if possible, readers who would desie to study a new Asian philosophy of Confucius and Kim Hang

2. The New Age and the New World

It is not told in his book when and how the new age and the new world will come. However, Kim Hang described the new world, the new heaven and earth, and the new human society that would come, following the universal laws. He explained the universal laws in the ancient Oriental terms of the ten *kan* (干, heavenly stems), the twelve *chi* (支, earthly branches), the sixty *kap ja* (甲子, sixty combinations of *kan* and *chi*), the sixty-four hexagrams (卦), yin and yang, the five elements (行), the eight trigrams, the *Ha Do* (Ho T'u, 河圖) Map, and the *Lak Seo* (Lo Shu, 洛書) Writing (James Legge, *The I Ching* [12]; Richard Willhelm, *The I Ching or Book of Changes* [21]). The universal laws seem to be fundamentally mathematical and truly beyond my comprehension. It seems to me that avatars, enlightened sages, understand the real meaning of the universal laws. I feel that the universal laws might correspond to the unknown (probably unknowable) laws of the whole, as the great physicist David Bohm said in his book *Wholeness and the Implicate Order* [3] (Lee Nichols, *The Essential David Bohm* [15]).

The ten *kan*, the twelve *chi,* and the sixty *kap ja* are used in lunar calendars to name the year, month, day, and hour of day. The use of these terms is quite convenient in handling and expressing these items, although there would be are variations in their names.

It is said in the bible, "In the beginning was the Word, and the Word was with God, and the Word was God. All things were made by him; and without him was not anything made that has been made" (John 1:1, 3).

In mathematics, the letters *e* and л are used as symbols to represent certain numbers that have special meaning. These Chinese characters or words seemingly represent information, facts, and truth. It seems to me that the *kan* and *chi* likewise are used to represent information, facts, and truth in lunar calendars in the Orient.

If all things predicted in the *Jeong Yeok* happened in the coming age of the later heaven, a month would be exactly thirty days and one year 360 days, expressed with integers without fractions. Integers can be seen in nature, such as the number of petals of beautiful flowers. It seems to me that the Earth, moon, and sun would mature, and then their movements would be expressed in integers too. The thirty days of the month and 360 days of the year are exactly multiples of ten, twelve, and sixty. Consequently, the names of the months and days of a year would be fixed if expressed in terms of *kan* (干) and *chi*.(支). For example, the first month of any year would be named *myo* (卯); New Year's Day, January 1, would be always named *kye mi* (癸未).

The first day of any month would be *kye mi* (癸未) or *kye chook* (癸丑); the sixteenth day of any month would be *moo jeen* (戊辰) or *moo sool* (戊戌) . The time of midnight of any day would be named *hae* (亥).

In the later heaven, the ten *kan* (干): *kap* (甲), *eul* (乙), *byung* (丙), *jeong* (丁), *moo* (戊), *ki* (己), *kyung* (庚), *sin* (辛), *yim* (壬), and *kye* (癸); the twelve *chi* (支): *ja* (子), *chook* (丑), *yin* (寅), *myo* (卯), *jeen* (辰), *sa* (巳), *oh* (午), *mi* (未), *shin* (申), *yoo* (酉), *sool* (戌), and *hae* (亥); and the sixty *kap ja* (甲子, combinations of *kan* and *chi)*, seem to be the best and the most appropriate terms or a priori words through the gate of which movements of the sun, Earth, and moon may be studied in the future calendar or astronomy of the solar system.

For example, the *ki* (己) position stands for the *Moogeuk* (无極, Wu Chi), the Non-Ultimate, the Creator God; the *moo* (戊) position stands for the *Hwanggeuk* (皇極, Huang Chi), the Ultimate Emperor, a sage. It seems to me that the positions *ki* and *moo* are non-local. The term "Original Heavenly Fire" (原天火) represents the creative power of the *Moogeuk*, the Creator God, and seems to express the infinite virtual energy of wholeness from the point of view of David Bohm's new quantum theories. The Original Heavenly Fire generates earth-soil (土) that seems to correspond to basic elements of matter. Yin and yang represent fundamental negative and positive forces such as the electromagnetic force, male and female, day and night, etc. The five *heng* (行)—earth-soil (土), metal (金), water (水), wood (木), and fire (火)—represent cosmic elementary, electromagnetic-like forces that seem to be "information," being creative with guiding principles, persistent, and changing. All things are created with the *Taegeuk* (太極, T'ai Chi), the Great Ultimate; yin-yang; and five elements (*heng*, 行); primordially by the *Moogeuk* (无極), the Creator God.

The Original Heavenly Fire generates earth-soil (土); earth-soil generates metal (金); metal generates water (水); water generates wood (木); wood generates fire (火); and fire generates earth-soil (土). It seems to me macroscopically and cosmologically imaginable and comparable to the above-described processes that a Big Bang (Stephen

Hawking), the Original Heavenly Fire (原天火) of an unknown form of energy would have generated a myriad of elemental particles composed of energy (earth-soil, 土): subatomic elements, quarks, antiquarks, photons, electrons, positrons, protons, neutrons, mesons, atoms, hydrogen, helium and so forth that contracted and eventually produced stars (the burning of helium producing carbon, nitrogen, and oxygen in the centers of stars), the sun, the Earth, and the moon. The earth-soil (土) would have generated metal (金)—metallic atoms, iron, copper, silver, gold, etc. Metal (金) then would have generated oceans and rainwater (水); water would have generated living organisms (木) that evolved into plants, animals, and finally man; and living organisms (木) would generate earth-soil (土) through decay or incineration with heat and fire (火).

The metal-to-fire change mentioned in the *Jeong Yeok* means extraordinary, unique, transitional changes from the earlier heaven to the later heaven that is predicted by transition from the *Lak Seo* (洛書, the Writing from the River Lo, the *River Writing*) to the *Ha Do* (河圖, the Yellow River Map, the *River Map*) (Figure 3).

The *Moogeuk* (无極, Wu Chi), expressed by the number ten, and the *Taegeuk* (太極, T'ai Chi), expressed by the number one, are oneness. All things are made by the *Moogeuk* and the *Taegeuk*. It seems to me that this relationship might be symbolically and mathematically imaginable as follows. A logarithm with a base of 1 is used:

$\text{Log } 1^0 = 0$

$\text{Log } 1^1 = 1$

$\text{Log } 1^2 = 2$

$\text{Log } 1^3 = 3$

$\text{Log } 1^n = n$

$\text{Log } 1^\infty = \infty$

$\text{Log } 1^\infty = \log 1 = 1$

$$\therefore \infty = 1$$

Therefore, $0 = 1 = \infty$. As David Bohm said, "All is in one; one is in all." God is immanent and transcendent. There is no separation. Separation is illusion. According to Paramahansa Yogananda (*To Be Victorious in Life* [26]), "your life, and all life, is governed with mathematical precision by God's intelligently framed cosmic laws." In the *Jeong Yeok*, $10 = \infty$; 10 is the Non-Ultimate; $10 = 1$; 10, the Non-Ultimate is oneness with 1, the Great Ultimate; $10 = 5$; the Non-Ultimate, 10, is oneness with the Ultimate Emperor, 5. The Numbers 10, 5, and 1 in the *Jeong Yeok* might be comparable with л and *e* alphabet letters in mathematics that indicate special infinite values and meanings, respectively.

The old preceding age and world ("the earlier heaven") are symbolically represented by the *Bok Hui* (伏羲) Eight Trigrams (the Fu Hsi Pa Kua, Figure 4) and the *Mun Wang* (文王) Eight Trigrams (the King Wen Pa Kua, Figure 5) and the *Lak Seo* (洛書) Writing (Figure 3) as well as the *Chou Yeok* (周易, *I Ching*). The coming new age and the new world ("the later heaven") are expressed by the symbol of the *Jeong Yeok* (正易) Eight Trigrams (Figure 6) and the *Ha Do* (河圖) Map (Figure 3) as well as the *Jeong Yeok* (the Third Yeok called by Jeong Ho Yi). The sets of eight trigrams are designed by different octagonal arrangements of eight trigrams.

The different diagrams of eight trigrams appear to symbolically imply historically active nations of the east, west, north, and south of the world in different ages. The old preceding age is characterized by being mutually destructive and the new age by being mutually supportive to life in humanity, as expressed by the *Mun Wang* (文王) and the *Jeong Yeok* (正易) Eight Trigrams, respectively.

If we carefully observe the *Mun Wang* (文王) Eight Trigrams (Figure 5), each trigram faces a trigram on the opposite side that is of the same gender, yin or yang in terms of number, with a feature of centrifugal expansion and growth, suggesting repulsion, as between two identical electromagnetic poles, further suggesting separation, disharmony, disorder, and mutual destruction in the earlier heaven. In contrary, in the *Jeong Yeok* (正易) Eight Trigrams (Figure 6), each trigram faces a trigram of the other gender, yin or yang in terms of number, with a feature of centripetal attraction, suggesting mutual attraction like electromagnetic attractive forces between two different poles, and further suggesting harmony, order, equality, cooperation, and mutual support in the coming later heaven.

These phenomena are also observable in the *Ha Do* (河圖) and the *Lak Seo* (洛書) (Figure 3). In the *Lak Seo,* 4-9 metal is in the south; 2-7 fire in the west; 1-6 in the north; and 3-8 wood in the east, indicating displacement of 4-9 and 2-7 from west and south, their original, correct positions in the *Ha Do*, respectively, suggesting disorder. Further, each of their numbers faces same gender number: 1-9, 2-8, 3-7, and 4-6, suggesting repulsion in the earlier heaven. In addition, the four odd heaven numbers 1, 3, 7, and 9 are at the middle positions of north, east, west, and south; the four even earth numbers 2, 4, 6, and 8 are at the corner positions of southwest, southeast, northwest, and northeast. These arrangements are suggestive of the suppression of yin and respect of yang in the earlier heaven. In the *Ha Do*, 4-9 metal and 2-7 fire return to west and south, their original, correct positions, respectively, indicating changes in their metal and fire positions; 1-6 water is in the north and 3-8 wood in the east, further showing perfect combinations of odd heaven numbers and even earth numbers in pairs in their arrangements of positions, suggesting attraction, maturation, completion, cooperation, peace, and mutual support in the coming later heaven.

Chou Yeok (周易, *I Ching*) is composed of the Text of the Sixty-Four Hexagrams and the Ten Wings (翼). *The I Ching* (James Legge, *The I Ching* [12]) existed in the time of Confucius. It is said that *the I*

Ching was originated by the Emperor Fu Hsi (伏羲), who lived about five thousand years ago, and that it was expanded with descriptions by King Wen (文王) and his son, the Duke of Chou (周). Confucius studied *the I Ching* in the late years of his life and added the Ten Wings (翼) of his commentaries to the existing *I Ching*.

Kim Hang was the first man in history who discovered that Confucius had foreseen the coming new *Jeong Yeok* (正易) Eight Trigrams and clearly described the specific octagonal arrangement of the eight trigrams, as illustrated in Figure 6. Kim Hang actually saw the completely new *Jeong Yeok* Eight Trigrams in a vision; it was yet unknown to scholars and not described in any books. Then he made efforts to search and find it in books, particularly in *the I Ching*. To his surprise, he found Confucius' description in the Discussion of the Trigrams (說卦傳), Chapter II (Jeong Ho Yi [23]; James Legge [12]; Richard Willhelm [21]). The words and sentences of Confucius' description of a new arrangement of eight trigrams were found to be understandable and explicated in view of the *Jeong Yeok* Eight Trigrams (Figure 6).

Confucius did not publicly mention the coming new world, but he foretold it in his writing in *the I Ching* as above described and believed it himself as Kim Hang wrote in *the Jeong Yeok*.

The I Ching begins with the hexagram *keon* (乾) and ends with the hexagram *mi jae* (未濟), for a total of sixty-four hexagrams. There are no description of the *Moogeuk* (无極) or *Hwanggeuk* (皇極) or the numbers ten and five in *the I Ching*. Ten is missing in the *Lak Seo* (洛書). Numbers one to ten are all present in *the Jeong Yeok*.

In *the Jeong Yeok,* it says that there are eight hexagrams: *bi* (否), standstill; *tae* (泰), peace; *sohn* (損), decrease; *ik* (益), increase; *ham* (咸), influence; *hang* (恒), duration; *ki jae* (既濟), after completion; and *mi jae* (未濟), before completion in description of the earlier and later heavens. In four hexagrams: heaven/earth *bi* (否), standstill; mountain/lake *sohn* (損), decrease; thunder/wind *hang* (恒), duration; and fire/water *mi jae* (未濟), before completion, trigrams that are supposed to be at the upper position exist above trigrams that are supposed to be at the lower positions, suggesting separation, repulsion, exclusion, exploitation, and mutual destruction in the earlier heaven without harmony or peaceful exchange. In the other four hexagrams, earth/heaven *tae* (泰), peace; lake/mountain *ham* (咸), influence; wind/thunder *ik* (益), increase; and water/fire *ki jae* (既濟), after completion, trigrams that are supposed to be at the upper positions move down and stay below those trigrams that are supposed to be at the lower positions and that move up above the other paired trigrams, suggesting attraction, exchange, cooperation, union, share, and mutual support in the later heaven. If the idea implied in the hexagram, earth/heaven *tae* (泰), peace is applied to economy in the later heaven, it might be inferred that the owner of a company truly supports his employees who would happily and voluntarily do their best in working with a feeling of themselves as like owners of the company. I would like to refer to Milai Industrial Company, in Japan that seems to suggest a possible example of an economic structure in a company in the later heaven [27].

The *yeok* (易) seems to be both metaphysical and physical science, especially astronomy, which describes and handles movements of the Earth, moon, sun, stars, and constellations.

Many stars and constellations were discovered by ancient Chinese scholars. Some major, important stars and constellations are represented and expressed by the ancient Chinese Twenty-Eight Lodges (宿), which is the oldest chart enduring up to this day, according to Frank Ross, Jr. (*Oracles, Bones, Stones and Wheelbarrows: Ancient Chinese Science and Technology* [18]).

A list of correlations between the names of the Twenty-Eight Lodges and the names of Western reference stars is available (Christopher Cull, *Astronomy and Mathematics in Ancient China: Zhou bi suan jing*; [5]; Frank Ross [18]). The celestial sphere of 360° is divided into twenty-eight divisions along the meridian in the Twenty-Eight Lodges (宿). For example, the star *Chin* (軫, "Axletree") corresponds to γ Corvi; *Jang* (張, "Spread") to μ Hydrae; *Sam* (參, "Triaster") to α Orionis; *Myo* (昴, "Mane") to 17 Tauri; *Shil* (室, "House") to η Pegasi; *Doo* (斗, "Dipper") to φ Sagittarii; *Sim* (心, "Heart") to α Scorpii; *Hang* (亢, "Gullet") to κ Virginis; and *Kak* (角, "Horn") to α Virginis.

The Twenty-Eight Lodges (宿, *Soo*) are included in the *Jeong Yeok* (正易). As Frank Ross wrote in his book *The Stars,* when American astronauts voyaged to the moon, the ancient Chinese equatorial-coordinate method was a key element in their system of navigation for the positioning of stars [18].

Figure 1 illustrates a star chart of the Twenty-Eight Lodges and corresponding Western reference stars. The second inner and the outermost circles show stars of the Twenty-Eight Lodges and corresponding Western reference stars, respectively. Positions of sun, Earth, moon, and stars are schematically drawn in a view from the north celestial pole. The rotation of the Earth, revolution of the moon around the Earth, and revolution of the Earth together with the moon around the sun are counterclockwise and indicated by arrows. The innermost circle indicates the location of the sun in each of the twelve months of a year, expressed by twelve *chi* (支). Winter and summer solstices and vernal and autumnal equinoxes (in the earlier heaven) are shown in parentheses. This illustration indicates the positions of sun, moon, and Earth on the first day *kye mi* (癸未) of the first month *myo* (卯), New Year's Day of every year (in the later heaven).

There seem to be some suggestions of astronomical or physical changes in the Earth, the solar system, and the universe during a possible transitional critical period from the earlier heaven to the later heaven; however, no discrete or concrete changes are presented by Kim Il Bu in his book *the Jeong Yeok* (正易).

3. *The Jeong Yeok,* 正易, *the Right Change* of 360 Days of a Year

In the new age, one month has exactly thirty days in each of the twelve months of the year. There will be exactly 360 days in each year, without leap years. There will be mild weather, like spring and autumn, without severely hot summer and severely cold winter.

The above prediction may suggest that Earth's axis stands vertical to the plane of the ecliptic with a vanishing of the 23.5 degree tilt of the Earth's axis and the celestial equator (the "Red Road") and the celestial ecliptic (the "Yellow Road") united, and that there would be no seasons (H. A. Rey, *The Stars* [16]). A twenty-four *chyul* calendar in which each month is divided into two *chyul* (節) is appended to *the Jeong Yeok*. Kim Hang claimed that *the Jeong Yeok, the Right Change* is the original calendar and will be ten thousand generations' calendar in the coming age. Barbara Clow wrote in her book *The Mayan Code* that the ancient Egyptians and Veda used a 360-day-year calendar five thousand years ago. To my knowledge, however, there seem to be no articles in the literature besides *The Mayan Code* that describe a year consisting of 360 days, except the appendix of *the I Ching* (The Great Treatise, Part I, Chapter IX; Jeong Ho Yi [8]; James Legge [12]; Richard Willhelm [21]), in which Confucius suggested that a year of the coming new age would contain 360 days!

Kim Hang clearly indicated that his Il Bu's one year of *the Jeong Yeok* exactly coincides with Confucius' one year of 360 days. It seems to me that the new age will bring the Kingdom of God on Earth, and that the universe, the solar system, sun, Earth, and moon will probably, in their correct movements, generating an originally God-planned correct movement of the revolution of Earth around the sun in exactly 360 days.

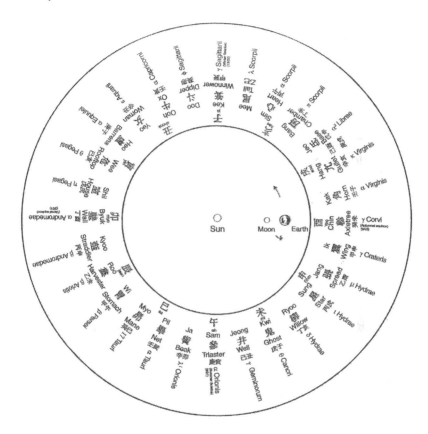

Figure 1. Star chart of the Twenty-Eight Lodges (宿, *Soo),* with corresponding Western reference stars. The middle and outer rings show the Twenty-Eight Lodges and corresponding Western reference stars, respectively. The rotation of the Earth, the revolution of the moon around the Earth, and the revolution of the Earth together with the moon around the sun are counterclockwise and indicated by arrows. The inner ring indicates the location of the sun in each of twelve months of a year, expressed by twelve *chi* (支, branches). Winter and summer

solstices and vernal and autumnal equinoxes (in the earlier heaven) are shown in parentheses (see text and notes 45, 52).

4. Relationship between the *Lak Seo* (洛書) Writing - *Ha Do* (河圖) Map and the *Mun Wang* (文王) - *Jeong Yeok* (正易) Eight Trigrams

The *Ha Do* and *Lak Seo* are originated as divine things according to Confucius' *I Ching* and Kim Hang's *Jeong* Yeok. The *Ha Do* and the *Jeong Yeok* Eightn Trigrams represent the later heaven; the *Lak Seo* and the *Mun Wang* Eight Trigrams represent the earlier heaven. In legends, the *Ha Do* Map was shown to *Bok Hui* (伏羲) with a dragon horse with a map of the *Ha Do* on its back coming out of the Yellow River; the *Lak Seo* Writing was shown to King *Woo* (禹) with a divine turtle with a writng of the *Lak Seo* on its back rising from the River Lo (Figure 3).

(1) The *Mun Wang* Eight Trigrams is based on the *Lak Seo*. There is a remarkable correlation and match between them as explained below.

The numbers 3, 4, 9, 2, 7, 6, 1 and 8 clockwis from east, south, west, and north in the *Lak Seo* completely correspond to those numbers in the *Mun Wang* Eight Trigrams with regard to the arrangement of trigrams and numbers. There is no division in pairs of 3-8, 4-9, 2-7, and 1-6 in arrangements in the *Lak Seo* and the *Mun Wang* Eight Trigrams, not like as seen in the *Jeong Yeok* Eight Trigrams as described below.

The four yang trigrams: *Keon* (乾, Ch'ien), *Kam* (坎, K'an), *Kan* (艮, Ken), and *Jin* (震, Chen) are situated in the yang region, north and east of the *Mun Wang* Eight Trigrams. The four yin trigrams: *Sohn* (巽, Sun), *Yi* (離, Li), *Kon* (坤, K'un), *Tae* (兌, Tui) are situated in the yin region, south and west of the *Mun Wang* Eight Trigrams.

Keon (乾) and *Kon* (坤), the father and mother are situated close to *Tae* (兌), the youngest daughter who needs the most patrents' care when she grows before maturity in the earlier heaven of growth, expansion, and disorder [23].

(2) According to Kim Hang, the later heaven of the *Jeong Yeok* Eight Trigrams based on the *Ha Do* Map will come after the earlier heaven represented by the *Mun Wang* Eight Trigrams, following unprecedented metal-fire change. This implies that 4 and 9 metal displaced in south of the *Mun Wang* Eight trigrams return to their right original positions, west of the *Ha Do* and the *Jeong Yeok* Eight Trigrams (before division of 4 and 9); 2 and 7 fire shift their positions from west of the *Lak Seo* and the *Mun Wang* Eight Trigrams to south, their original right positions in the *Ha Do* and the *Jeong Yeok* Eight Trigrams (before division of 2 and 7) These shifts of positions indicate the **Metal Fire Change** predicted by Kim Hang in his book.

In contrary to that pairs of 3-8, 4-9, 2-7 and 1-6 show no division and remain side by side in the *Lak Seo* and the *Mun Wang* Eight Trigrams, pairs of 3-8, 2-7, 4-9, and 1-6 divide, 3 yang number moves to the yin region of west; 8 yin number remains in the yang region of east in the *Jeong Yeok*; 2 yin number moves to the yang region of north; 7 yang number moves to the yin region of south; 1 yang number moves to the yin region of sountheast; 6 yin number moves to the young region of northwest. These movements reflect and exactly coincide with the change from the heaven/earth *bi* (否) trigram of the earlier heaven to the earth/heaven *tae* (泰, peace) trigram of the later heaven, showing that the young upper trigram, heaven, in the upper young region goes down to the lower yin region, and the lower yin trigram, earth, goes up to the upper young region, indicating influence each other and peaceful exchange in the later heaven.

The four young trigrams: *Kan* (艮), *Kam* (坎), Keon (乾), and *Jin* (震) are located in the young region of east, northeast, north, and northwest ; the four yin trigrams: *sohn* (巽), *Kon* (坤), *Yi* (離), and *Tae* (兌) are located in the yin region of southeast, south, southwest, and west. *Keon* (乾) and *Kon* (坤), the father and mother stand in the middle of the eight trigrams in north and south, symbolizing parental governance. *Kan* (艮) and *Tae* (兌) are situated in east and west, symbolizing great leading roles in humanity in the later heaven. *Jin* (震) and *Sohn* (巽), the oldest son and daughter stand beside *Keon* (乾) and *Kon* (坤), the father and mother and assist their parents in the later heaven.

The *Bok Hui* Eight Trigrams represents the first trigrams of birth; the *Mun Wang* Eight Trigrams represents the second trigrams of growth after birth. The *Jeong Yeok* Eight Trigrams represents the third trigrams of maturity and completion of the later heaven, and further predicts the establishment of the Kingdom of God on Earth as in heaven. Both of the *Mun Wang* and *Bok Hui* Eight Trigrams existed at the time of Confucius and their arrangements of the two trigrams are described in the Confucius' Commentaries to the *I Ching* but explanation of the relationship between the *Ha Do-Lak Seo* and the two eight trigrams are not presented in *the I Ching*.

There is another description of third, undetermined eight trigrams besides the above two in Confucius' Commentaries. Kim Hang was the first scholar who discovered that the third unknown eight trigrams written by Confucius in *the I Ching* represented the *Jeong Yeok* Eight Trigrams which he saw in his vision. Confucius then appeared in his vision and congratulated Kim Hang for his achievement of establishing the third *Jeong Yeok* Eight Trigrams, and confirming its truth.

5. Emergence of Maitreya Buddha in the New World

Kim Hang predicted in his book that the future Buddha, Maitreya (彌勒, *Miruk*), would be in the new world and the new age of *Yong-Hwa* (龍華歲月), the "Dragon-Flower Era". Maitreya Buddha will teach humanity.

Gautama Buddha predicted in his sermon that Maitreya Buddha would be the coming future Buddha. He preached that when Maitreya Buddha comes to the world, the light of the Maitreya's body will spread over the entire world (*Anagatavamsa Desana: The Chronicle-to-Be,* translated by Udaya Meddegama [14]; Jacky Sach, *The Everything Buddhism Book* [19]; Jeong Ho Yi [25]; Sogyal Rinpoche, *The Tibetan Book of Living and Dying* [17]).

So'taesan (1891–1943) was the master of *Won* Buddhism in Korea. He foretold to his disciples in his sermon the coming of the future Buddha Maitreya and the Dragon-Flower Era (Bongil Chung, *The Scriptures of Won Buddhism* [4]). In the Dragon-Flower Era of Maitreya Buddha, So'taesan said-"Human intelligence will be far advanced, so that there will be no antagonism or conflicts in the human world. The hearts of the people will be as follows: Whereas people today regret when they cannot take another's property by force, defeat or hurt others, people in the coming world will be worried when they cannot give to others, lose to others or help others. Whereas today's individuals, families, societies and nations defend themselves by erecting fences and walls, there will be harmony without limitation in the coming world. Whereas people today are ruled by material civilization, people in the coming world will control material civilization with strengthened spiritual culture, as they will have a highly advanced morality. .....Korea will be the leader of all countries in the world as far as morality is concerned."

Alice A. Bailey, the author of the book *The Reappearance of the Christ* [1], wrote about a prediction of the coming of Maitreya Buddha. Maitreya the Christ will have physical presence on Earth (Christ is a Greek word meaning the Messiah). He will be Dispenser of Water of Life. He will be Nutrisher of the little ones of humanity. He will unify the East and the West throughout the world, irrespective of religion and nationality. Maitreya the Christ cares not what the faith is if the objective is love of God and of humanity. He will come to work for the Plan of God that is to establish the Kingdom of God on Earth; our Father will be present on Earth as in heaven."

According to Bailey, right human relation is taught and established in every aspect of daily living family life, communal life, governmental action, and all people of the entire field of international relations. The Law of Reincarnation, the Law of Evolution, and the Law of Cause and Effect (the Law of Karma) are taught. In the coming new world, mysteries in science hidden in nature and planetary energies and forces will be unlocked and controlled by human minds, providing enormous usefulness to humanity. Divine knowledge in the greatest spiritual science will be revealed. All men and women have divinity; the principle of sharing will control economic affairs with love and justice in humanity.

It is my belief that Maitreya Buddha is the *Huanggeuk* (皇極), the Ultimate Emperor. The *Hwanggeuk* and the *Moogeuk* (无極), the Non-Ultimate are oneness as shown in the Kim Hang's *Jeong Yeok* 正易 [8, 23]. Buddhists seek truth through the *Hwanggeuk*, Buddha that leads to the *Moogeuk*, the Creator God. Christians seek truth through the *Moogeuk*, God that leads to the *Hwanggeuk*, son of God, Jesus. Christians also seek truth through Jesus Christ who is the *Hwanggeuk* (author's belief) that leads to God, the *Moogeuk*. Therefore, Buddhism and Christianity appear to be two different religions but essentially oneness. Confucianism with *the Jeong Yeok* seems to be a connecting bridge between Buddhism and Christianity. Budhism, Christianity, and Confucianism seem to be fundamentally oneness. Paul Knitter, Professor of Theology, World Religions and Culture at Union Theological Seminary, in New York, wrote in his book *Without Buddha I Could Not Be a Christian* that he can be a Christian only by also being a Buddhist, and that he is a Buddhist Christian [9]. Gautama Buddha,

Maitreya Buddha, Jesus Christ, Confucius, Kim Hang, Muhammad, and Paramahansa Yogananda are believed to represent the *Hwanggeuk* (皇極), the Ultimate Emperor, son of God who achieved Buddha nature or divine nature (fully revealing the super self). I believe that all major religions of the world seem to be different paths but they all lead to the mountaintop of the Creator, God and that they are truly oneness. All men and women have Buddha nature, divinity within as their super-self (see author's book, *Seeking a New World* [6].

6. Prediction of the Presence of Our Father God in the New World

Kim Hang predicted that the Kingdom of Heaven would be founded on the Earth and our Supreme God would be present in glorious radiance on Earth as in heaven as it is prophesied in the Bible that the Lord will be in a new heaven and a new earth (Old Testament Isaiah 65: 17-25; New Testament Revelation 21:1-27).

The Creator God is expressed as the *Moogeuk* (无極, Wu Chi), the Non-Ultimate, and is represented by the number ten in the *Jeong Yeok*. Action, or the process of activity of the *Moogeuk* in its beginning is expressed by the *Taegeuk* (太極, T'ai Chi), the Great Ultimate and represented by the number one. The number five, halfway between ten and one, represents the *Hwanggeuk* (皇極, Hwang Chi), the Ultimate Emperor that expresses man, sage, or son of God. All the other things of the universe are represented by the other numbers, two through nine. The real meaning of this numerology is unknowable to ordinary people.

It may be inferred that the *Taegeuk* (太極), the Great Ultimate, might be the ultimate essence of quanta, the root of energy and consciousness enfolded in quanta. The *Taegeuk* seems to be "Word" (logos-principle, (理), and possibly "information" of David Bohm that is action (用) of the *Moogeuk* and has creative energy (氣). The universe is the manifestation of God's Word.

In *the Jeong Yeok,* it is said that in the macrocosm there are three *weon* (元), origins: the *Moogeuk*, the Non-Ultimate; the *Hwanggeuk*, the Ultimate Emperor; and the *Taegeuk*, the Great Ultimate or heaven, man, and earth. It seems to me inferable that in the microcosm—that is, in a human being—there are three selves: the super self, the inner self, and the physical self, as described in the Chapters 5 to 7 of the author's book *Seeking a New World* [6]; they seem to most likely correspond to the *Moogeuk*, the *Hwanggeuk*, and the *Taegeuk* in *the Jeong Yeok,* and the *Three-Body Doctrine* (Trikaya) in Mahayana Buddhism: "the physical body *(Nirmanakaya),* the enjoyable body (*Sambhogakaya*), and the essence body (Dharmakaya) [9], respectively. The physical self and body are originated from the *Taegeuk* (太極), the Great Ultimate, and developed with the principles of yin and yang as female and male, and the five elements (行, heng). The inner self is created by and from the *Moogeuk* (无極), the Non-Ultimate, becoming the *Hwanggeuk* (皇極), the Ultimate Emperor. The super self would be part of the *Moogeuk*. Man is believed to represent a union of the *Moogeuk*, the *Hwanggeuk*, and the *Taegeuk* (see the author's book *Seeking a New World* [6]).

7. The New Civilization of the New World

The light of God will gloriously illuminate heaven and earth. The sun and moon will brightly shine. A glossy, beautiful world will be born. The Yellow River will once become clean. Correct human relations, propriety (called 禮, *ye*), and beautiful music (樂) will prevail in human society in the coming later heaven.

The I Ching and *the Jeong Yeok* predict that the ending and the recommencing of all the things of the world will be accomplished in the nation *Kan* (艮) of the east, which is expressed by the Eight

Kan (a symbol of a mountain) in the diagram of the *Jeong Yeok* Eight Trigrams.

Kan (艮, Ken) is situated in northeast in the *Mun Wang* (文王) Eight Trigrams, suggesting that all things of human history of the earlier heaven that began in *Jin* (震, Chen) in the east will come to an end in the Nation *Kan* (艮). After metal and fire change their positions in the *Lak Seo* (洛書) that is basis of the *Mun Wang* (文王) Eight Trigrams, moving to the original positions in the *Ha Do* (河圖) that is the basis of the *Jeong Yeok* (正易) Eight Trigrams, *Kan* (艮) moves to its correct position in the east and will start all things of the later heaven.

Confucius said in the Discussion of the Trigrams (設卦傳), describing the future *Jeong Yeok* (正易) Eight Trigrams, "Therefore: Water and fire complement each other, thunder and wind do not interfere with each other, and the forces of mountain and lake are united in their action. Thus only are change and transformation possible, and thus only can all things come to perfection." (Richard Willhelm *the I Ching or Book of Changes* [21], Jeong Ho Yi [23, 25]).

The Nation *Kan* (艮, Ken) of the east will unite with the Nation *Tae* (兌, Tui) of the west, expressed by the "Three *Tae*" (a symbol of a lake), and interchange their influences; that is, the spiritual culture of the East and the scientific civilization of the West will harmoniously join; thereafter, they will be able to change and transform human society and nations, and to give completion to all things in humanity, making enormous contributions to the coming of the new age and the new world. It is believed by students of the Kim Hang's philosophy that the *Kan* (艮) in the *Jeong Yeok* (正易) Eight Trigrams indicates an Eastern nation, being very suggestive of Korea as a leading country of the East, and that the *Tae* (兌) indicates a Western nation, being very suggestive of America as a main country of the West. Then the East and the West will unite and become one world under the heavens. The *Jeong*

Yeok (正易) calendar will be used internationally, replacing lunar and solar calendars. The Kingdom of God will be established on the Earth. The Father, the Supreme God, will be present on Earth as in heaven. There is a remarkable complete agreement between both predictions by Kim Hang in the East and by Alice Bailey in the West concerning the establishment of the Kingdom of God on Earth as in heaven as well as emergence of Maitreya Buddha. Humanity will become one family under heaven, enjoying peace, justice, sharing, and happiness with brotherhood and sisterhood. Goodness will be boundless in humanity. The civilization of the new world is unimaginable.

Christianity (represented by Jesus Christ) and Confucianism (represented by Confucius and Kim Hang) seem to teach the same thing about the new age and the foundation of the Kingdom of God on Earth that is the plan of God and the will of God, giving humanity boundless hope.

I humbly and respectfully write the above sacred stories, seeking a true new world and praying to God for his grace and love.

January 5, 2008

Sung Jang Chung
(聖貫 鄭聖璋)
Nashville, Tennessee
U.S.A.
December 15, 2009

26

The Jeong Yeok 正易

The Book of Right Change

Written by Kim Hang

Translated by Sung Jang Chung

10 and 5 and 1 Word [1]

Oh, *Bango* (盤古)[2] did change; the Heaven Emperor had nothing to do.

The Earth Emperor carried virtue; the Human Emperor worked.

Yuso (有巢, You Chao) already built a house; Soo In (燧人, Sui Ren) then invented fire.

Godly *Bok Hui* (伏羲, Fu Hsi) drew the Eight Trigrams and made straw-knotted cords[3]; Holy Shin Nong (神農, Shen Nung) plowed fields and held a market.

Hwang Jye (黃帝, Huang Di), the Yellow Emperor created sixty *kap ja* (甲子), combinations of *kan chi* (干支), stem and branch; and observed stars and the Northern Dipper; God-like Yo (堯, Yao) made a calendar of day and month, and was enthroned in year *kap jeen* (甲辰).

The Emperor Soon (舜, Shun) made an observatory equipment, *Okhyung* (玉衡) and implemented administration of seven-day week.

Our Great Emperor Woo (禹, Yu) drained flood water off the land and divided the country in nine *choo* (疇, districts); then a marvelous turtle with the Writing of the *Lak Seo* (洛書) on its back rose out of the River Lo.

In the shrine of the country *Eun* (殷) can virtue be observed.

29

Ki Sung (箕聖, Ji Sheng) was a sage[4]; virtue of the country Chou (周) was here; songs of *Yinam*; (二南) and *Chilwol* (七月) praised virtue of King Wen (文王) and the Duke of Chou (周公).

Giraffe-like, our sage Confucius stood in the middle of the age *keon* (乾) and *kon* (坤) ; he inherited the preceding age and transferred it down, transferred it to today.

Oh, today and today; 63, 72 and 81 become 1 with Il Bu (一夫).

Extending all fingers, then that is the *Moogeuk* (无極, Wu Chi), the Non-Ultimate 10[5].

Counting 10 with one finger, then it indicates the *Taegeuk* (太極, Tai Chi), the Great Ultimate 1[6].

If 1 has no 10, it has no *chyae* (體), body, structure[7]; if 10 has no 1, it has no *yong* (用), action, function[8]; if 10 and 1 unite, they become earth-soil (土)[9].

Halfway is 5, it is the *Hwanggeuk* (皇極, Huang Chi), the Ultimate Emperor.

The earth carries the heaven and is square, so it is the body (體).

The heaven envelopes the earth and is round, so it is the shadow (影).

How great the *tao* (道), way of body and shadow is!

Yi (理), logos-principle and *ki* (氣), energy reside; spiritual divinity is immanent[10].

Yi (理), logos-principle of heaven and earth is 3 *weon* (元), origins: the *Moogeuk* (无極, Wu Chi), the Non-Ultimate, the *Hwanggeuk* (皇極, Huang Chi), the Ultimate Emperor, and the *Taegeuk* (太 極, Tai Chi), the Great Ultimate.

The *weon* (元), origin, the *Moogeuk* (无極), the Non-Ultimate sent down sages; it showed them the divine things, that is, the *Ha Do* (河圖) Map and the *Lak Seo* (洛書) Writing[11].

The *yi* (理), logos-principle of the *Ha Do* (河圖) and the *Lak Seo* (洛書) is the later heaven and the earlier heaven.

The *tao* (道), way of the heaven and earth is *ki jae* (既濟), after completion and *mi jae* (未濟), before completion.

The Dragon Map, the *Ha Do* (河圖), is the image of *mi jae* (未濟), before completion and *do seng* (倒生), falls and is born; and *yeok seong* (逆成), reverses and matures[12]. It becomes the earlier heaven, the *Taegeuk* (太極), the Great Ultimate[13].

The Turtle Writing, the *Lak Seo* (洛書) is the number of *ki jae* (既濟), after completion and *yeok seng* (逆生), reverses and is born and *do seong* (倒成), falls and matures; it becomes the later heaven the *Moogeuk* (无極), the Non-Ultimate[14].

Five is in the middle position and the *Hwanggeuk* (皇極), the Emperor Ultimate.

The *yeok* (易) reverses; when it comes to an ultimate end, it will return.

Earth-soil comes to an ultimate and generates water. Water comes to an ultimate and generates fire; fire comes to an ultimate and generates metal. Metal comes to an ultimate and generates wood. Wood comes to an ultimate and generates earth-soil. Earth-soil generates fire.

Metal and fire change their residences. It is a principle of *do yeok* (倒逆), falls and reverses.

Oh, how supreme it is, the *Moogeuk* (无極) of the *Moogeuk* (无極). Confucius did not say it.

Not saying words and believing with faith are the Confucius' *tao* (道), way[15].

He was fond of the *yeok* (易) in the late period of his life. He wrote ten Wings (翼), commentaries to the *yeok* (易). His *tao* (道), way was penetrated with one. Truly, Confucius is our teacher of ten thousands of generations[16].

If heaven is 4, earth is 6.

If heaven is 5, earth is 5.

If heaven is 6, earth is 4.

The number of heaven and earth ceases at 10.

10 is *kee* (紀), order and 2 is *kyung* (經), longitude.

5 is *kang* (綱), rule and 7 is *wee* (緯), latitude.

The *moo* (戊) position where the stem is smooth and the number reverses, and its number attains perfection at 32 degree. It is the mother of the later heaven water metal *Taeeum* (太陰), the Great Yin.

The *ki* (己) position where the stem reverses and the number is smooth, its number attains perfection at 61 degree. It is the father of the earlier heaven fire wood *Taeyang* (太陽), the Great Yang.

The Great Yin is reverse born and falls to mature. It is the earlier heaven and the later heaven, and *ki jae* (既濟) and *mi jae* (未濟).

The Great Yin is spirit (魂) of 1 water and ghost (魄) of 4 metal (being a source of water and metal). It is fertilized at the moo (戊) position, the first degree when the moon is in conjunction with the sun. It is developed at 9 degree. It is nourished at 13 degree.

It is born at 21 degree. The degree attains completion at 30.

It ends at the *ki* (己) position, the first degree when the year attains perfection. It returns at the *moo* 戊 position, 11 degree when the year attains perfection.

The *yi* (理), logos-principle of return is 1, 8 and 7.

Five days are 1 *hoo* (候); 10 days are 1 *ki* (氣); 15 days are 1 *chyul* (節); 30 days are 1 month; 12 months are 1 year.

The Great Yang falls to be born and reverse matures. It is the later heaven and the earlier heaven, and *mi jae* (未濟), before completion and *ki jae* (既濟), after completion.

The Great Yang is *ki* (氣), energy of 7 fire and *chae* (體), body of 8 wood (being a source of energy for all living things). It fertilizes at the *ki* (己) position, 7 degree when the sun attains completion. It develops at 15 degree. It is nourished at 19 degree. It is born at 27 degree. The degree attains completion at 36.

It ends at the *moo* (戊) position, 14 degree when a year completes the degree. It returns to the *ki* (己) position, the first degree when a year completes the degree.

The *yi* (理), logos-principle of return is 1, 7 and 4.

15 minutes are 1 *kak* (刻); 8 *kak* (刻) are 1 *shi* (時, 2 hours); 12 *shi* (24 hours) are 1 day.

> Heaven and earth unite virtue; it is 32.
>
> Earth and heaven unite *tao* (道), way; it is 61.
>
> The sun and moon share the palace; non-existing earth exists.
>
> The moon and sun share the degree; they precede the later heaven.
>
> The moon of the earlier heaven of 36 palace greatly illuminates the 30 days of the later heaven.

The degree of the divided bodies of 4 *sang* (象), images is 159[17].

The expanded number of 1 *weon* (元), origin is 216.

The later heaven administers at the earlier heaven; it is water/fire *ki jae* (既濟), after completion.

The earlier heaven administers at the later heaven; it is fire/water *mi jae* (未濟), before completion.

Metal Fire First Hymn[18]

A sage bestows *tao* (道), way ; metal and fire become clear.

A general moves counting sticks for strategy; water and land become calm.

A peasant washes a hoe; he gets a good harvest.

A painter sets aside the brush; *roe poong* (雷風) is born[19].

A virtue reaches the Heaven Emperor; it can not be named[20].

A joyful melody brings an auspicious phoenix singing.

An auspicious phoenix sings; it sounds like *yool ryeo* (律呂), heaven and earth sounds[21].

Metal Fire Second Hymn[22]

The great *tao* (道), way of our *Hwanggeuk* (皇極), the Emperor Ultimate reaches heaven's mind. *Ki* (氣), energy of north and east firmly keeps positions[23]. *Yi* (理), logos-principle of west and south passes through each other [24].

Kyung (庚) metal is 9 and its energy (氣) is filled. *Jeong* (丁) fire is 7 and its number is vacant.

Execution of mutual change of metal and fire positions represents operation of the changing power of heaven and earth.

Wind (*Sohn*, 巽) and cloud (*Kam,* 坎) move at numbers 1 and 4, and sang (象) .

Song and music shine in military merit and literary virtue.

It is a joy that the Yellow River once becomes clean.

It is a pleasure to see an Il Bu's grand spectacle.

A crane breathes wind at the Eight *Kan* (艮) Mountain in east.

A white stork changes at the Three *Tae* (兌) Lake in west; it is a scenery.

Looking at this is a great magnificence.

There are three thousand *ye* (禮), right human relations, propriety; and righteousness is one.

Metal Fire Third Hymn[25]

With clean wind blowing from the northern window, harmonizing with musical tone from Yun Myung's (淵明) stringless harp, gradually climbing the first eastern mountain of the 3-8 *Kan* (艮, Ken), I clearly realize the meaning of our Confucius saying: "The Lou (魯) Country is small."

Taking the head band off, hanging it on a stone, looking toward south, a blue pine tree puts a shelf across a short hollow[26]. In front of the mountain of the western borderland, a white heron is flying.

Leisurely shaking a white feather fan, looking down at the Red Wall River, red and red, white and white, in the middle of them, there is a person studying Confucianism, Taoism and Buddhism. He is playing a flute and enjoying the bright moon.

Metal Fire Fourth Hymn

The 4, 9, 2, 7 metal-fire gate is a place which ancient people's thoughts did not reach.

I become its owner and gradually open it[27]. 1 and 6 in north, and 3 and 8 in east are divided in left and right[28]. The world shown by *the Jeong Yeok* (正易) is a great magnificent scenery through all ages and all places.
It is a most spectacular view of all ages.

Singing and praising one verse of the *Chilwol* (七月), July Chaper[29], greatly adoring the holy virtue of the Duke of Chou (周公), alas, what Confucius did not say is today!

Metal Fire Fifth Hymn

Oh, metal and fire exchange each other; *yeok* (易) becomes the changeless *Jeong Yeok* (正易). *Hoe* (晦), the last day of month; *sak* (朔), the fist day of month; *hyun* 弦, the day with a half moon; *mang* (望), the 15th day with a full moon; *cheen* (進), advance; *toi* (退), retreat; *gool* (屈), bend; *shin* (伸), extend; degree of *yool yeo* (律呂), and merit and *yong* (用), action of creation stand.

That is what sages did not say. How should Il Bu dare to say it?

35

However, it is the time to say and there is a heaven's order.

Oh, the virtue of the sun and moon is the minute of heaven and earth.

1 minute multiplied by 15 equal 1 *kak* (刻) .

1 *kak* (刻) multiplied by 8 equal 1 *shi* (時) .

1 *shi* (時) multiplied by 12 equal 1 day.

1 day multiplied by 30 equal 1 month.

1 month multiplied by 12 equal 1 year.

1 year is born to month; 1 month is born to day; 1 day is born to *shi* (時).

1 *shi* (時) is born to *kak* (刻) ; 1 *kak* 刻 is born to minute; 1 minute is born to emptiness. Emptiness has no position[30].

A year of the Emperor Yo (堯) is 366 days.

A year of the Emperor Soon (舜) is 365 ¼ days.

A year of Il Bu is 375 degrees; if 15 is respected as emptiness and subtracted from 375, it equal 360 degrees; 360 exactly coincide with our Confucius' one year, that is, 360 days of a year.

At 5 degrees, spirit of the moon, its illuminated surface is born at *shin* (申)[31]; it is the third day of month.

The moon shows the illuminated upper half surface at *hae* (亥); it is the 8th day.

The body of the moon matures at *oh* (午), showing the full bright surface; it is the 15th day, *mang* (望) and the earlier heaven[32].

The moon divides at *sool* (戌); it is the 16th day[33].

The moon shows the illuminated lower half surface at *sa* (巳); it is the 23rd day.

The moon declines at *jeen* (辰); it is the 28th day.

The moon returns at *ja* (子); it is the 30th day of month, *hoe* (晦), and the later heaven.

The moon unites at the middle position of the middle palace; the first day is *sak* (朔).

6 water and 9 metal gather and expand and become *yool* (律).

2 fire and 3 wood divide and become shadow and *yeo* (呂).

Yool Yeo (律 呂) Degree of One Year Revolution

In minutes, it is 12,960.

In *kak* (刻), it is 864.

In *shi* (時), it is 108.

In days, it is 9.

The logos-principle gathers at the origin; the origin is the nature.

In the middle of *keon* and *kon* (乾 坤) and heaven and earth are *roe* (雷), thunder and *poong* (風), wind.

Year *kap shin* (甲申, 1884), June 26th day, *moo sool* (戊戌), I revised and praised.

Water and earth-soil attain *tao* (道), way and become heaven and earth.

Heaven and earth unite virtue and become the sun and moon.

The Great Yang (太陽) is constant; *seong* (性), nature is perfect; and *yi* (理), logos-principle is straight.

The Great Yin (太陰) wanes and waxes; number fills; and *ki* (氣), energy vacates.

What fills and vacates is *ki* (氣), energy; it is the earlier heaven.

What wanes and waxes is *yi* (理), logos-principle; it is the later heaven.

Tao (道), way of the later heaven is bending and stretching.

Administration of the earlier heaven is advance and retreat.

Administration of advance and retreat is that the moon fills and vacates.

Tao (道), way of bending and stretching is that the moon wanes and waxes.

Suppressing yin and respecting yang is a law of mind of the earlier heaven[34].

Adjusting yang and matching yin is a *tao* (道), way of nature and logos-principle of the later heaven [35].

Heaven and earth are an empty shell without the sun and moon.

The sun and moon are a vacant shadow without a supreme man.

Yi (理), logos-principle of ebb and flow is that 1, 6 *yim kye* (壬 癸) water take a position in north; 2, 7 *byung jeong* (丙丁) reside in south.

Fire energy (氣) flames up. Water nature (性) goes down.

They mutually impact, mutually advance and retreat, and follow *shi* (時) , *hoo* (候), *ki* (氣) and *chyul* (節) ; it is administration of the sun and moon.

Oh, administration of the sun and moon!

It is extremely mysterious and extremely bright. It can not be described with writing.

Alas, what does heaven say? What does earth say? Il Bu (一夫) can say.

Il Bu (一夫) can say!

Tidewater rises in southern heaven in the morning; tidewater flows out of northern land in the evening.

When water flows out of the northern land, it is difficult to tell morning or evening.

Water/fire *ki jae* (旣濟), after completion becomes fire/water *mi jae* (未濟), before completion.

Great *tao* (道), way comes from heaven; heaven does not say.

Geat virtue comes from earth; earth follows words.

Heaven 1 *yim* (壬) water bends ten thousand times and surely flows toward east.

Earth 1 *ja* (子) water bends ten thousand times and follows *yim* (壬) water.

Year *kap shin* (甲申, 1884), *ryoohwa* (流火) June 7th day

Great Sage Seven *Weon Goon* (元君) writes.

Oh, if heaven and earth do not say, does Il Bu (一夫) say anything?

Heaven and earth say, so Il Bu (一夫) dares to say.

Heaven and earth say that Il Bu (一夫) should say.

Il Bu (一夫) says what heaven and earth say.

How great the metal-fire gate is!

Heaven and earth go in and out; and Il Bu (一夫) goes in and out.

So it is a gate of three *jae* (才, power).

Energies of the sun, the moon, stars and the Northern Dipper come to light. Il Bu's *ki* (氣), energy comes to light; it is a 5 weon (元), origin gate.

Eight wind blows and Il Bu (一夫) wind blows.

So it is the gate of the 10 *Moo* (无), Nothingness, the 10 *Moogeuk* (无極).

> The sun and moon greatly illuminate the residence of *keon kon* (乾坤).
>
> Heaven and earth see the magnificent view of *roe poong* (雷風), thunder wind palace[36].
>
> Who knows that the returning up moon of the earlier heaven straightly illuminates the palace of birth of metal-fire day?

Hwa Moo Sang Jye (化无上帝), the Supreme Emperor, the Creator God's Word[37].

On returning up and arising, the moon reaches the heaven's center, returning to conjunction with the sun. The moon meets the heaven's center.

On coming to the *hwang choong* (皇中), the emperor's middle and arising, the moon meets the *hwang sim* (皇心), the emperor's center[38].

Ancient people dared to often mention about the moon. How often would it return up and meet the heaven's center?

The moon rises and returns up, and then becomes the heaven's center moon.

The moon arises in the *hwang choong* (皇中), the emperor's middle; and becomes the *hwang sim* (皇心), the emperor's center moon.

The *Hwa Ong* (化翁), the Creator God's mind that broadly creates a heaven, surely instructs the *hwang choong* (皇 中), the emperor's middle moon.

Hwa Ong (化翁), the Creator God's Repeated Word

In reasoning and expanding, do not possibly violate right morality.

If you fall and lose heaven's reason, the parent's mind will be in danger.

How could an unworthy son dare to figure out reason and number; I only wish to ease the parent's mind[39].

Year *kap shin* (甲申, 1884), July 17th day *ki mi* (己未), an unworthy son, Kim Hang (金恒) is moved to tears and respectfully writes

Hwa Ong (化翁), the Creator God Himself Showing Changing Things.

Oh, metal and fire rightly change; *bi* (否)[40], standstill goes and *tae* (泰)[41], peace comes.

Oh, *ki* (己) position himself administers, *moo* (戊) position becomes respected emptiness.

Oh, *chook* (丑) palace prospers, *ja* (子) palace retreats position[42].

Oh, *myo* (卯) palace works, *yin* (寅) palace declines position.

Oh, five w*oon* (運), movement operates and six *ki* (氣),energy moves. 10 and 1 become one body; merit and virtue are boundless.

Degree of Body Position of the *Moogeuk* (无極), the Non-Ultimate

Kisa sa (己巳) *moo jeen* (戊辰) *ki hae* (己亥) *moo sool* (戊戌).

The degree (度) of *kan chi* (干支), stem and branch reversely goes from *ki* (己) to *moo* (戊) and the number smoothly goes from 10 to 5. The number of completion is 61.

Degree of Body Position of the *Hwanggeuk* (皇極), the Empror Ultimate

Moo sool (戊戌) *ki hae* (己亥) *moo jeen* (戊辰) *ki sa* (己巳).

The degree (度) of *kan chi* (干 支), stem and branch smoothly goes from *moo* (戊) to *ki* (己) and the number reversely goes from 5 to 10. The number of completion is 32.

Degree of Body Position of the Moon-*geuk* (月極), the Moon Ultimate (The Great Yin)

Kyung ja (庚子) *moo shin* (戊申) *yim ja* (壬子) *kyung shin* (庚申) *ki sa* (己巳) .

The first 1 degree exists but does not exist.

5 days are 1 *hoo* (候).

And the number of completion is 30.

Degree of Body Position of the Sun-*geuk* (日極), the Sun Ultimate (The Great Yang)

Byung oh (丙午) *kap yin* (甲寅) *moo oh* (戊午) *byung yin* (丙寅) *yim yin* (壬寅) *sin hae* (辛亥).[

The first 1 degree does not exist but exists.

On the 7th day, it returns.

And the number of completion is 36.

Hwa Ong (化翁), the Creator God has no position[43]. He is the original heaven fire[44]. He generates 10 *ki* (己), earth-soil.

Ki sa (己巳) palace is the earlier heaven and the later heaven.

Earth 10 *ki* (己) earth-soil generates heaven 9 *sin* (辛) metal.

Heaven 9 *sin* (辛) metal generates earth 6 *kye* (癸) water.

Earth 6 *kye* (癸) water generates heaven 3 *eul* (乙) wood.

Heaven 3 *eul* (乙) wood generates earth 2 *jeong* (丁) fire.

Earth 2 *jeong* (丁) fire generates heaven 5 *moo* (戊) earth-soil.

Moo sool (戊戌) palace is the later heaven and the earlier heaven.

Heaven 5 *moo* (戊) earth-soil generates earth 4 *kyung* (庚) metal

Earth 4 *kyung* (庚) metal generates heaven 1 *yim* (壬) water.

Heaven 1 *yim* (壬) water generates earth 8 *kap* (甲) wood.

Earth 8 *kap* (甲) wood generates heaven 7 *byung* (丙) fire.

Heaven 7 *byung* (丙) fire generates earth 10 *ki* (己) earth-soil.

Earth 10 *ki* (己) earth-soil generates heaven 9 *kyung* (庚) metal.

Heaven 9 *kyung* (庚) metal generates earth 6 *kye* (癸) water.

Earth 6 *kye* (癸) water generates heaven 3 *kap* (甲) wood.

Heaven 3 *kap* (甲) wood generates earth 2 *byung* (丙) fire.

Earth 2 *byung* (丙) fire generates heaven 5 *moo* (戊) earth-soil.

Heaven 5 *moo* (戊) earth-soil generates earth 4 *sin* (辛) metal.

Earth 4 *sin* (辛) metal generates heaven 1 *yim* (壬) water.

Heaven 1 *yim* (壬) water generates earth 8 *eul* (乙) wood.

Earth 8 *eul* (乙) wood generates heaven 7 *jeong* (丁) fire.

Heaven 7 *jeong* (丁) fire generates earth 10 *ki* (己) earth-soil.

Earth 10 *ki* (己) earth-soil matures heaven 1 *yim* (壬) water.

Heaven 1 *yim* (壬) water matures earth 2 *jeong* (丁) fire.

Earth 2 *jeong* (丁) fire matures heaven 9 *sin* (辛) metal.

Heaven 9 *sin* (辛) metal matures earth 8 *eul* (乙) wood.

Earth 8 *eul* (乙) wood matures heaven 5 *moo* (戊) earth-soil.

Heaven 5 *moo* (戊) earth-soil matures earth 6 *kye* (癸) water.

Earth 6 *kye* (癸) water matures heaven 7 *byung* (丙) fire.

Heaven 7 *byung* (丙) fire matures eath 4 *kyung* (庚) metal.

Earth 4 *kyung* (庚) metal matures heaven 3 *kap* (甲) wood.

Heaven 3 *kap* (甲) wood matures earth 10 *ki* (己) earth-soil.

Byung (丙), *kap* (甲), and *kyung* (庚), 3 palaces are heaven and earth of the earlier heaven.

Jeong (丁), *eul* (乙), and *sin* (辛), 3 palaces are earth and heaven of the later heaven.

The earlier heaven is of 3 heavens and 2 earths[5, 6].

The later heaven is of 3 earths and 2 heavens[5, 6].

Ja (子), *yin* (寅), *oh* (午), and *shin* (申) are the earlier and later heaven of the earlier heaven.

Chook (丑), *myo* (卯), *mi* (未), and *yoo* (酉) are the earlier and later heaven of the later heaven.

Kan Chi (干支) **Diagram of Upper** *Weon* (元) *Chook Hoi* (丑會)

Ki chook (丑) palace is *kyung yin* (庚寅), *sin myo* (辛卯), *yim jeen* (壬辰), *kye sa* (癸巳), *kap oh* (甲午), *eul mi* (乙未), *byung shin* (丙申), *jeong yoo* (丁酉), *moo sool* (戊戌).

Ki hae (己亥) palace is *kyung ja* (庚子), *sin chook* (辛丑), *yim yin* (壬寅), *kye myo* (癸卯), *kap jeen* (甲辰), *eul sa* (乙巳), *byung oh* (丙午), *jeong mi* (丁未), *moo shin* (戊申).

Ki yoo (己酉) palace is *kyung sool* (庚戌), *sin hae* (辛亥), *yim ja* (壬子), *kye chook* (癸丑), *kap yin* (甲寅), *eul myo* (乙卯), *byung jeen* (丙辰), *jeong sa* (丁巳), *moo oh* (戊午).

Ki mi (己未) palace is *kyung shin* (庚申), *sin yoo* (辛酉), *yim sool* (壬戌), *kye hae* (癸亥), *kap ja* (甲子), *eul chook* (乙丑), *byung yin* (丙寅), *jeong myo* (丁卯), *moo jeen* (戊辰) .

Ki sa (己巳) palace is *kyung oh* (庚午), *sin mi* (辛未), *yim shin* (壬申), *kye yoo* (癸酉), *kap sool* (甲戌), *eul hae* (乙亥), *byung ja* (丙子), *jeong chook* (丁丑), *moo yin* (戊寅) .

Ki myo (己卯) palace is *kyung jeen* (庚辰), *sin sa* (辛巳), *yim oh* (壬午), *kye mi* (癸未), *kap shin* (甲申), *eul yoo* (乙酉), *byung sool* (丙戌), *jeong hae* (丁亥), *moo ja* (戊子).

Turning Energy Diagram of The 28 *Soo* (宿), Lodges (Constellations)[45]

Kye mi (癸未)	Chin (軫)	*Kye chook* (癸丑)
Kap shin (甲申)	Ik (翼)	*Kap yin* (甲寅)
Eul yoo (乙酉)	Jang (張)	*Eul myo* (乙卯)
Byung sool (丙戌)	Sung (星)	*Byung jeen* (丙辰)
Jeong hae (丁亥)	Ryoo (柳)	*Jeong sa* (丁巳)
Moo ja (戊子)	Kwi (鬼)	*Moo oh* (戊午)
Ki chook (己丑)	Jeong (井)	*Ki mi* (己未)
Kyung yin (庚寅)	Sam (參)	*Kyung shin* (庚申)
Sin myo (辛卯)	Ja (觜)	*Sin yoo* (辛酉)
Yim jeen (壬辰)	Pil (畢)	*Yim sool* (壬戌)
Kye sa (癸巳)	Myo (昴)	*Kye hae* (癸亥)
Kap oh (甲午)	Wi (胃)	*Kap ja* (甲子)
Eul mi (乙未)	Roo (婁)	*Eul chook* (乙丑)
Byung shin (丙申)	Kyoo (奎)	*Byung yin* (丙寅)
Jeong yoo (丁酉)	Byuk (壁)	*Jeong myo* (丁卯)
Moo sool (戊戌)	Shil (室)	*Moo jeen* (戊辰)
Ki hae (己亥)	Wee (危)	*Ki sa* (己巳)
Kyung ja (庚子)	Heo (虛)	*Kyung oh* (庚午)
Sin chook (辛丑)	Yeo (女)	*Sin mi* (辛未)
Yim yin (壬寅)	Ooh (牛)	*Yim shin* (壬申)
Kye myo (癸卯)	Doo (斗)	*Kye yoo* (癸酉)
Kap jeen (甲辰)	Kee (箕)	*Kap sool* (甲戌)
Eul sa (乙巳)	Mee (尾)	*Eul hae* (乙亥)
Byung oh (丙午)	Sim (心)	*Byung ja* (丙子)
Jeong mi (丁未)	Bang (房)	*Jeong chook* (丁丑)
Moo shin (戊申)	Jeo (氐)	*Moo yin* (戊寅)
Ki yoo (己酉)		*Ki myo* (己卯)

Kyung sool (庚戌)   *Kyung jeen* (庚辰)

Sin hae (辛亥)   Hang (亢)   *Sin sa* (辛巳)

Yim ja (壬子)   Kak (角)   *Yim oh* (壬午)

Poem of Respecting Emptiness of the Two *Soo* (宿), Lodges, *Hang* (亢) and *Kak* (角)

What can hear the sound of *kak* (角)? Divinity is Jeo (氐); *Hang* (亢) can not follow it.

36 degrees from *Shil* (室) to *Jang* (張) are vast and boundless.

Military merit is drug that eases stomach[46]. Literal virtue is medicine that nourishes mind[47]

The principle of metal and fire is rightly clarified. The sounds of *Yool Yeo* 律呂 harmonizes yin and yang.

9 and 9 Reciting

All fluent and elegant Confucian scholars may listen to me reciting a song.

Reading *Seo Jeon* (書傳, *Book of History*) and studying *Yeok* (易, *the I Ching*) are things of the earlier heaven.

Reasoning truth and cultivating morality. Who does these things in the later heaven?

Our Confucius who loved reading *the I Ching* and broke leather thongs of the book three times, did not say of the *Moogeuk* (无極), the Non-Ultimate but had it in his mind.

Il Bu (一夫) who has been crazy for his whole life of 60 years laughs by himself and others laugh; there are constantly many laughs. There are laughs among laughs. What laughs does he laugh? He can laugh the laugh, and laughs and sings.

360 days are a year; the great *weon* (元, root) that is the number 300 is arranged in 9 and 9 counting: the *moo moo* (无无, nothing and nothing) position that is the number 60 is divided and spread in the 1, 6 palace. If single 5 is taken as empty and subtracted from 60, 55 points are bright. If 15 is taken as empty and subtracted from 60, 45 points are mottled.[48]

Probably, the right truth and the deep mysterious true scripture are present in this palace. Indeed, if with sincere will and righteous mind, one studies all the time with no laziness, surely, our *Hwa Hwa Ong* (化化翁), the Creator God will certainly endow teaching; this is to like what I like, is it not?

10 and 5 Song

Water/fire becomes *ki jae* (既濟); fire/water becomes *mi jae* (未濟).
Ki jae (既濟) becomes *mi jae* (未濟); heaven and earth are 3 *weon* (元).
Mi jae (未濟) becomes *ki jae* (既濟); heaven and earth are 5 *weon* (元).
Heaven/earth becomes earth/heaven; 3 *weon* (元) becomes 5 *weon* (元).
3 *weon* (元) becomes 5 *weon* (元); upper *weon* (元) becomes weon *weon* (元 元).

Upper *weon* (元) becomes *weon weon* (元元); 10 and 5 say 1 word; 10 and 5 say 1 word; metal and fire change.

Metal and fire change; a calendar of ten thousands of generations is drawn.

A calendar of ten thousands of generations is drawn; lake/mountain *ham* (咸) is thunder/wind *hang* (恒).

Lake/mountain *ham* (咸) is thunder/wind *hang* (恒); it is 10 and 5.

Right and Leap Degrees of the Earlier and Later Heavens

In the earlier heaven, the square is made the body (體) and the round is made the action (用); on the 27th first day of month comes a leap month[49] .

In the later heaven, the round is made the body (體) and the square is made the action (用); 360 days become a right year. The original heaven is boundless.

Degrees of Revolution of the Earlier and Later Heavens

The earlier heaven is 216 ten thousand *li* (里) .

The later heaven is 324 ten thousand *li* (里) .

The sum of the earlier and later heavens is 540 ten thousand *li* (里).

From *Bango* 5th *hwa* (化) first year yim yin (壬寅) to *Daechung* (大淸) *Kwangseo* (光緖) 10th year *kap shin* (甲申) (1884) is 118,643 years[50].

At my age of 36 years I followed my teacher Yeon Dam, (蓮潭).

He bestowed me a pen name Kwan Byuk (觀碧). He gave me a stanza and said:

In viewing clearness, nothing is clearer than water (*kye hae* 癸亥).

To like virtue, one should do *in* (仁, love-benevolence).

The image of moon moves at the heaven's center moon.

I would like to advise you to seek this truth.

Poem of Establishing *Tao* (立道), Enlightenment

I quietly looked at a blue sky changing in ten thousand ways.

At my age of 54 years (1879) I accomplished my study for the first time.

Marvelous, marvelous, subtle, subtle; marvelous and subtle truth is in nothingness, nothingness, and existence, existence, in the middle of existence and nothingness.

Poem of Nothingness Position (无位)

Tao (道), way is divided in three; its reason is natural.

The three are Confucianism, Buddhism and Taoism.

Who knows that Il Bu (一夫) truly mastered these.

If no man is available, I will keep it, and if available, I will transfer it to him.

Year *kap shin* (甲申), month *byung ja* (丙子), day *moo jeen* (戊辰) 28th, I write and revise.

Poem of Jeong Yeok (正易)

Number of heaven and earth is number of counting the sun and moon.

If the sun and moon are not right, *yeok* (易) is not *yeok* (易).

Yeok (易) becomes *the Jeong Yeok* (正易), the Right Change; only then *yeok* (易) becomes *yeok*(易).

Why does the original *yeok* (易) use a leap *yeok* (易)?

Poem of Spreading Map[51]

An everlasting writing shines like the sun and moon.

In a page of a map, thunder and wind are born.

I quietly look at the nothing-middle-blue of the universe.

Who knows that heaven's work awaits man to accomplish it?

Diagram of the Metal Fire *Jeong Yeok Do* (金火正易圖)[52]

金火正易圖

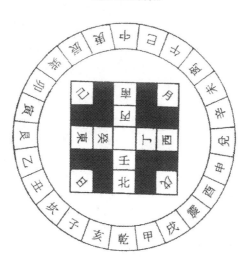

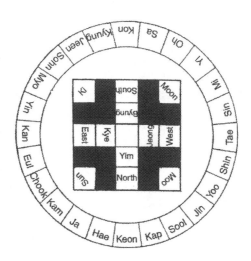

Figure 2. Diagram of Metal Fire *Jeong Yeok Do* (金火正易圖). The upper diagram is the original diagram of Metal Fire *Jeong Yeok Do* (金火正易圖). The lowere is a translated diagram. The outer ring is divided in 24 divisions (see text and notes).

10 and 1 Saying 1 Word

Earth-soil of 10 and water of 6 are unchangeable earth.

Water of 1 and earth-soil of 5 are unchangeable heaven.

Heavenly administration opens at *ja* (子). Earthly administration opens at *chook* (丑).

Chook (丑) *woon* (運), movement is 5 and 6. *Ja* (子) *woon* (運), movement is 1 and 8[53].

1 and 8 are number of arising shadow of the returning up (復上) moon.

5 and 6 are number of maturing body of *hwang choong* (皇中), the emperor's middle moon.

9, 7, 5, 3 and 1 are odd numbers.

2, 4, 6, 8 and 10 are even numbers.

Odd and even numbers are two five. The former five are heaven *tao* (道), way. The latter five are earth virtue.

The order of 1, 3 and 5 is to measure heaven.

The order of 7 and 9 is to count earth. There are three heavens and two earths.

Heaven/earth *bi* (否) becomes earth/heaven *tae* (泰); *tae* (泰) is the later heaven and *bi* (否) is the earlier heaven.

Yeok (易) of the earlier heaven is *yeok* (易) of exchanging yeok (易) (the *Bok Hui* (伏羲) Eight Trigrams).

Yeok (易) of the later heaven is *yeok* (易) of changing *yeok* (the *Mun Wang* (文王) Eight Trigams).

Yeok (易) changes to the 9 palace, the *Mun Wang* (文王) Eight Trigrams, and *yeok* (易) changes to the *Jeong Yeok* (正易) Eight Trigrams.

Yi (離, Li) and *keon* (乾, Ch'ien) of the *Bok Hui* (伏羲) Eight Trigrams are numbers 3 and 1 that are in the right positions of east and north in the *Mun Wang* (文 王) Eight Trigrams.

Kam (坎, K'an) and *kon* (坤, K'un) of the *Bok Hui* (伏羲) Eight Trigrams are numbers 6 and 8 that are at the corners of north and east in the *Mun Wang* (文王) Eight Trigrams.

Tae (兌, Tui) and *Kan* (艮, Ken) of the *Bok Hui* (伏羲) Eight Trigrams are numbers 2 and 7 that are at mutual positions of west and south in the *Mun Wang* (文王) Eight Trigrams.

Jin (震, Chen) and *sohn* (巽, Sun) of the *Bok Hui* (伏羲) Eight Trigrams are numbers 10 and 5. They are heads of the 5 heng (行), elements, and the first son and daughter of six children.

10 and 5 take the middle positions and generate *the Jeong Yeok* (正易).

Kyung (庚) and *sin* (辛) of *kan* (干), stems are 9 and 4 of numbers that are in south in the *Mun Wang* (文王) Eight Trigrams, exchanging west positions.

Number of Birth and Maturation of the *Lak Seo* (洛書) 9 Palace

Heaven 1 generates *yim* (壬) water and earth 1 matures *ja* (子) water.

Heaven 3 generates *kap* (甲) wood and earth 3 matures *yin* (寅) wood.

Heaven 7 generates *byung* (丙) fire and earth 7 matures *oh* (午) fire.

Heaven 5 generates *moo* (戊) earth-soil and earth 5 matures *jeen* (辰) earth soil.

Sool (戌) 5 is empty.

Heaven 9 generates *kyung* (庚) metal and earth 9 matures *shin* (申) metal.

3 *Weon* 元 Number of Division and Combination of 3 and 5

At midnight of *kap* (甲) and *ki* (己), *kap ja* (甲子) is born; *byung yin* (丙寅) becomes head[54].

At midnight of *eul* (乙) and *kyung* (庚), *byung ja* (丙子) is born; *moo yin* (戊寅) becomes head.

At midnight of *byung* (丙) and *sin* (辛), *moo ja* (戊子) is born; *kyung yin* (庚寅) becomes head.

At midnight of *jeong* (丁) and *yim* (壬), *kyung ja* (庚子) is born; *yim yin* (壬寅) becomes head.

At midnight of *moo* (戊) and *kye* (癸), *yim ja* (壬子) is born; *kap yin* (甲寅) becomes head.

Number of Birth and Maturation of the *Ha Do* (河圖) Eight Trigrams

Earth 10 generates *ki* (己) earth-soil and heaven 10 matures *chook* (丑) earth-soil.

Earth 4 generates *sin* (辛) metal and heaven 4 matures *yoo* (酉) metal.

Earth 6 generates *kye* (癸) water and heaven 6 matures *hae* (亥) water.

Earth 8 generates *eul* (乙) wood and heaven 8 matures *mi* (未) wood. *Myo* (卯) 8 is empty.

Earth 2 generates *jeong* (丁) fire and heaven 2 matures *sa* (巳) fire.

5 *Weon* (元) Number of Division and Combination of 9 and 2

At midnight of *ki* (己) and *kap* (甲), *kye hae* (癸亥) is born; *jeong myo* (丁卯) becomes head[55].

At midnight of *kyung* (庚) and *eul* (乙), *eul hae* (乙亥) is born; *ki myo* (己卯) becomes head.

At midnight of *sin* (辛) and *byung* (丙), *jeong hae* (丁亥) is born; *sin myo* (辛卯) becomes head.

At midnight of *yim* (壬) and *jeong* (丁), *ki hae* (己亥) is born; *kye myo* (癸卯) becomes head.

At midnight of *kye* (癸) and *moo* (戊), *sin hae* (辛亥) is born; *eul myo* (乙卯) becomes head.

Poem of 10 and 1 Returning Body

Fire enters metal country and metal enters fire.

Metal enters fire country and fire enters metal.

Fire metal becomes metal fire. It is the original heaven way (道) .

Who has sent the Dragon-Flower Age of Maitreya Buddha to now?

Administrative order is *ki* (己), *kyung* (庚), *yim* (寅), *kap* (甲) and *byung* (丙).

Yeo Yool (呂律) is *moo* (戊), *jeong* (丁), *eul* (乙) *kye* (癸) and *sin* (辛).

Earth 10 becomes heaven and heaven 5 is earth.

To *myo* (卯) returns *chook* (丑) and on *sool* (戌) depends s*hin* (申).

10 is the middle of 19.

9 is the middle of 17.

8 is the middle of 15.

7 is the middle of 13.

6 is the middle of 11.

5 is the middle of 9.

4 is the middle of 7.

3 is the middle of 5.

2 is the middle of 3.

1 is the middle of 1.

The middle is emptiness of 10 and 10, 1 and 1.

It is the middle of Yo (堯) and Soon's (舜) "that middle".

It is the middle of Confucius' "middle in time".

It is Il Bu's position of so-called enveloping 5 and including 6, and where 10 retreats and 1 advances.

Little son, clearly listen to my saying one word, little son.

Number of Action and Administration of Thunder (雷) and Wind (風) Right Position

Ki (己) position is the middle of 4 metal, 1 water, 8 wood, 7 fire; it is the *Moogeuk* (无 極), the Non-Ultimate [52,56]

It is the *Moogeuk* (无極), the Non-Ultimate and the *Taegeuk* (太 極), the Great Ultimate; and 10 and 1, indicating oneness of both ultimates[6, 9, 52].

10 and 1 are earth virtue and heaven way (道).

Heaven way (道) is round, and *kyung* (庚), *yim* (寅), *kap* (甲) and *byung* (內).

Earth virtue is square, and 2, 4, 6 and 8.

Moo 戊 position is the middle of 2 fire, 3 wood, 6 water, 9 metal, and the *Hwanggeuk* (皇 極, the Emperor Ultimate)[52,57].

It is the *Hwanggeuk* (皇極, the Ultimate Emperor) and the *Moogeuk* (无極, the Non-Ultimate;), and 5 and 10[52.]

5 and 10 are heaven degree and earth number.

Earth number is square and *jeong* (丁), *eul* (乙), *kye* (癸) and sin (辛).

Heaven degree is round and 9, 7, 5, 3.

Number of Using Middle of 4 Right & 7 *Soo* (宿), Lodges

The earlier heaven is 5, 9, reversely goes and uses 8. It goes wrong and is adjusted with a leap *yeok* calendar.

The later heaven is 10, 5, smoothly goes and uses 6. It agrees and is matched with the *Jeong* Yeok (正易).

5 to 9 are administration of the Geat Yin; they are 1, 8 and 7.

10 to 5 are administration of the Geat Yang; they are 1, 7 and 4.

Yeok is 3[58], and *keon* (乾) and *kon* (坤).

Hexagrams are 8: *bi* (否), standstill; *tae* (泰), peace; *sohn* (損), decrease; *ik* (益), increase; *ham* (咸), influence; *hang* (恒), duration; *ki jae* (既濟), after completion, and *mi jae* (未 濟), before completion.

Oh, already smooth [59] and already reverse[60], it can end and begin[61].

The 10 *yeok* (易) of the *Jeong Yeok* (正易) is the calendar of ten thousands of generations.

10 and 1 Reciting

10 and 1 become one body, and 5 and 8 are respected emptiness.

5 and 8 are respected emptiness, and 9 and 2 are divided and combined[62].

9 and 2 are divided and combined, and fire shines and metal clears.

Fire shines and metal clears, and heaven and earth are clear and bright.

Heaven and earth are clear and bright, and the sun and moon brightly shine.

The sun and moon brightly shine, and there is a glossy world.

The world and world come together, and the Supreme Lord is present radiantly.

The Supreme Lord is present radiantly, and people are joyful and happy.

People are joyful and happy, and all things are right and just.

All things are right and just, and good and good, goodness is boundless.

Eul yoo (乙酉 year, 1885), *kye mi* (癸未) month, *eul mi* (乙未) day 28th an unworthy son, Kim Hang (金恒) respectfully writes[63].

The Ha Do   河   圖

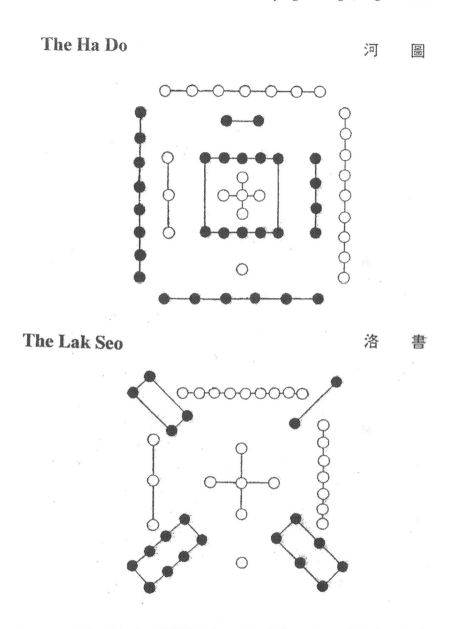

The Lak Seo   洛   書

Figure 3. The *Ha Do* (河圖) Map (the Yellow River Map) and the *Lak Seo* (洛書)) Writing (the Writing from the River Lo). The upper diagram is the *Ha Do* (河圖) Map and the lower is the *Lak Seo* (洛書) Writing (see text and notes).

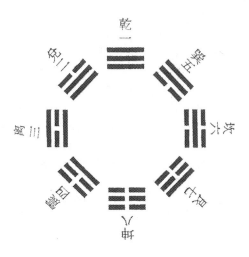

伏羲八卦圖

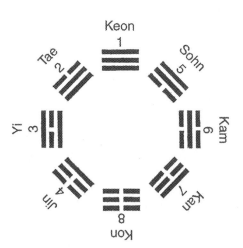

Figure 4. Diagram of the *Bok Hui* (伏羲, Fu Hsi) Eight Trigrams. The upper diagram is the original diagram and the lower is a translated one (see text and notes).

文王八卦圖

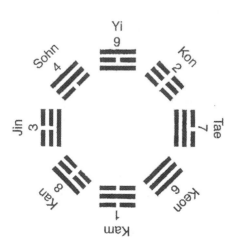

Figure 5. Diagram of the *Mun Wang* (文王, King Wen) Eight Trigrams. The upper diagram is the original diagram and the lower is a translated one (see text and notes).

正易八卦圖

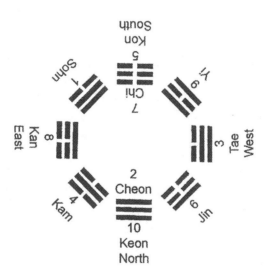

Figure 6. Diagram of the *Jeong Yeok* (正 易) Eight Trigrams. The upper diagram is the original diagram and the lower is a translated one (see text and notes).

十干原度數

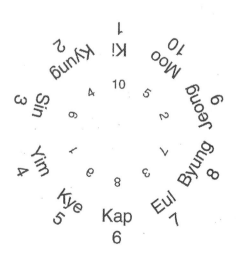

Figure 7. Diagram of Original Degree of Ten *Kan* (干). The upper diagram is the original diagram and the lower is a translated one (see text).

Climate Degree of 12 months 24 *Chyul* (節)

Myo (卯) month 3rd day *eul yoo* (乙酉) *yoo* (酉) right 1 *kak* (刻) 11 minute *won hwa* (元和)

18th day *kyung ja* (庚子) *ja* (子) right 1 *kak* (刻) 11 minute *choong hwa* (中化)

Jeen (辰) month 3rd day *eul myo* (乙卯) *myo* (卯) right 1 *kak* (刻) 11 minute *dae hwa* (大和)

18th day *kyung oh* (庚午) *oh* (午) right 1 *kak* (刻) 11 minute *po hwa* (布化)

Sa (巳) month 3rd day *eul yoo* (乙酉) *yoo* (酉) right 1 *kak* (刻) 11 minute *roe hwa* (雷和)

18th day *kyungja* (庚子) *ja* (子) right *1 kak* (刻) 11 minute *poong hwa* (風化)

Oh (午) month 3rd day *eul myo* (乙卯) *myo* (卯) right 1 *kak* (刻) 11 minute *ip hwa* (立和)

18th day *kyung oh* (庚午) *oh* (午) right 1 *kak* (刻) 11 minute *heng hwa* (行化)

Mi (未) month 3rd day *eul yoo* (乙酉) *yoo* (酉) right 1 *kak* (刻) 11 minute *keon hwa* (建和)

18th day *kyung ja* (庚子) *ja* (子) right 1 *kak* (刻) 11 minute *bo hwa* (普化)

Shin (申) month 3rd day *eul myo* (乙卯) *myo* (卯) right 1 *kak* (刻) 11 minute *chung hwa* (清和)

18th day *kyung oh* (庚午) *oh* (午) right *1 kak* (刻) 11 minute *pyung hwa* (平化)

Yoo (酉) month3rd day *eul yoo* (乙酉) *yoo* (酉) right 1 *kak* (刻) 11 minute *sung hwa*(成和)

18th day *kyung ja* (庚子) *ja* (子) right 1 *kak* (刻) 11 minute *yip hwa* (入化)

Sool (戌) month 3rd day *eul myo* (乙卯) *myo*(卯)right1 *kak* (刻)11 minute *ham hwa*(咸和)

18th day *kyung oh* (庚午) *oh* (午) right 1 *kak* (刻) 11 minute *hyung hwa* (亨化)

Hae (亥) month 3rd day *eul yoo* (乙酉) *yoo* (酉) right1*kak* (刻)11 minute *jeong hwa* (正和)

18th day *kyung ja* (庚子) *ja* (子) right 1 *kak* (刻) 11 minute *myung hwa* (明化)

Ja (子) month 3rd day *eul myo* (乙卯) *myo* (卯) right 1 *kak* (刻) 11 minute *chi hwa* (至和)

18th day *kyung oh* (庚午) *oh* (午) right 1 *kak* (刻) 11 minute *jyung hwa* (貞化)

Chook (丑) month 3^{rd0}day *eul yoo*(乙酉)*yoo* (酉) right 1 kak(刻)11 minute *tae hwa*(太和)

18th day *kyung ja* (庚子) *ja* (子) right 1 *kak* (刻) 11 minute *chae hwa* (體化)

Yin (寅) month 3rd day *eul myo* (乙卯) *myo*(卯) right 1 *kak* (刻) 11 minute *yin hwa* (仁和)

18th day *kyung oh* (庚午) *oh* (午) right 1 *kak* (刻) 11minute *seong hwa* (性化)

THE GREAT *YEOK* FOREWORD (大易序)

Holy is the *yeok* (易) that is *yeok* 易. *Yeok* (易) is the calendar.

Without the calendar there is no sage. Without a sage there is no calendar.

Therefore, it is the reason why the first original *yeok* (the *Bok Hui* 伏羲) *Yeok* and the coming *yeok* (*the Jeong Yeok* 正易) are made.

The Confucius' personal writing (ten commentaries in *the I Ching*) is cherished by me. *Tao* (道), way penetrates beyond heaven and earth.

Bok Hui (伏羲, Fu Hsi) simply drew the *Bok Hui* (伏羲) Eight Trigrams and *Mun Wang* (文王) elaborated the *Mun Wang* (文王) Eight Trigrams. Heaven and earth have been declining in danger for 2,800 years.

Oh, holy, the Confucius' sacredness! A sage who knows heaven is a sage.

A sage who enjoys heaven is a sage. A sage who devotedly served heaven as his parent is only the sage Confucius.

Clearly looking at the formless realm of heaven and earth can be done by Il Bu (一夫).

Thorough mastery of the formed *yi* (理), logos-principle of heaven and earth has been preceded by Confucius.

Oh, holy, the Confucius' sacredness!

The head of literature is Conggu (孔丘, Confucius). The head of politics is Mengga (孟軻, Mencius). Oh, both teachers! They are eternal sages.

Il Bu's (一夫) Facts

His origin is the eternal *Hwa Moo Ong* (化无翁), the Creator God of heaven and earth.

His ancestry is a descendant of the 37th king of *Silla* (新羅) dynasty.

The origin is beyond limits and the ancestry long.

He is spiritually enlightened on the formless realm beyond heaven and earth.

Who has seen truth of the first *weon* 元, origin of heaven and earth is probably Kim Il Bu (金一夫).

Il Bu's (一夫) Vestage

His family has accumulated virtue for 3,000 years and got the supreme luck throughout heaven and earth. God told the above.

His merit of 60 years of cultivation of nature and his grasping justice will be greatly revealed as the years go by. These are instructions from above.

Il Bu (一 夫) respectfully write. May I hopefully escape from sin? *Sin sa* (辛巳, 1881), June 22nd day Il Bu (一夫)[64].

Notes

(1) It is saying (word) that 10, the Non-Ultimate (无極, Wu Chi), 5, the Ultimate Emperor (皇極, Huang Chi), and 1, the Great Ultimate (太極, Tai Chi) unite and are oneness [8, 23].

(2) *Bango* (盤古) is believed to mean the Creator God [8, 23].

(3) Nets and baskets were used in hunting and fishing [8, 21].

(4) Ki Sung (箕聖) is Ki Ja (箕子, Ji Zi).

(5) Finger-counting is used in operation of *kan* and *chi* (干支, stem and branch). Extending all fingers means here to extend the thumb to count 10 next from 9, opening all fingers of the left hand when counting from 1 to 10, by starting bending the thumb (1) in an opened hand (reverses and is born), then the index finger (2), the middle finger (3), the ring finger (4), and the little finger (5), and next to extend the little finger (6), the the ring finger (7), the middle finger (8), the index finger (9), and last the thumb (10) (falls and matures). This finger- counting is in the way of increasing numbers (reverse, 逆).

(6) Counting 10 means bending the thumb in an open hand when counting 10, at starting in an open left hand, bending the thumb (10) (falls and is born), the index finger (9), the middle finger

(8), the ring finger (7), the little finger (6), next extending the little finger (5), the ring finger (4), the middle finger (3), the index finger (2), last the thumb (1) (reverses and matures).. This finger counting is the way of decreasing numbers (falls, 倒). Therefore, the bent thumb indicates 10 in the falling counting and simultaneously one in the reverse counting, indicating the Great Ultimate 1. In finger-counting, the thumb represents 10 and 1, symbolizing that the Non-Ultimate, 10 is simultaneously the Great Ultimate, 1, as written in *the Jeoong Yeok,* indicating that the Non-Ultimate and the Great Ultimate are oneness. The fifth finger represents 5 and 6, reflecting a statement of "enveloping 5 and including 6"of 1 and 6 palace in *the Jeong Yeok* [8]. Fingers and their numbers in counting with a left hand indicate three ultimates and are employed in calculative operation and reasoning in *the Jeong Yeok.* This procedure is difficult to comprehend for the author but seems to have metaphysical unknown grounds like unknown laws of movement of the wholeness described by David Bohm [3, 15].

If the thumb, the third, and the fifth fingers are raised (bent) in an open left hand and indicate three yin numbers, 10, 8, and 6 in "heaven" (yang region in finger-counting), these numbers match those in the yang region of north (10), east (8), and northwest (6) in the *Jeong Yeok* Eight Trigrams, and two extended second and fourth fingers indicate yang numbers 9 and 7 in "earth" (yin region in finger-counting) match those in the yin region of southwest (9) and south (7) in the *Jeong Yeok* Eight Trigrms. If the second and fourth fingers are raised (bent) and indicate 2 and 4, and the thumb, third, and fifth fingers are extended in "earth" and indicate 1, 3, and 5 (in yin region), numbers 2 and 4, and 1, 3, and 5 then match those numbers in yang region of north (2) and northeast (4), and in yin region of southeast (1), west (3), and south (5) in the *Jeong Yeok* Eight Trigrams, respectively. There are "three heavens and two earths" in counting 10 to 6; there are "two heavens and three earths" in counting 5 to 1 if expressions in the *jeong Yeok* are followed. It seems to me remarkable that there are correlations in relations between the *Ha Do* and the finger-counting with regard to the *Jeong Yeok* Eight Trigrams.

If the thumb, third, and fifth fingers are raised (bent), and 5 and 10 are not taken in consideration because the two numbers are missing in the *Mun Wang* Eight Trigrams, then the fingers show that 1, 3, 8, and 6 are in heaven (yang region), exactly agreeing with those numbers in north, east, northeast, and northwest (yang region) in the *Mun Wang* Eight Trigrams; the fingers also show that 2, 9, 4, and 7 are in earth (yin region), exactly agreeing with those numbers in southwest, south, southeast, and west (yin region) in the *Mun Wang* Eight Trigrams.

(7) *Chae* (體), body or structure seems to correspond to substance of the wholeness, the totality that carries out enfolding and unfolding. David Bohm referred to the wholeness and described in his new quantum theories [3, 15].

(8) *Yong* (用), action or function of the *chae* (體), body or structure seems to correspond to process (enfolding and unfolding) of the wholeness, the totality that is described by David Bohm [3, 15].

(9) Earth-soil seems to not only indicate soil but also the Earth as a whole.

(10) All things are composed of logos-principle and energy, together with spiritual divinity within. It is inferred that the physical body and physical self of man are composed of logos-principle (physical and chemical laws) and energy (matter), and that the spiritual divinity exists as the inner/super self (true self) within the physical body/physical self of man. It seems to the author that the Darwin's theory of evolutionism might be applicable in the realm of the

physical body/physical self of man, and that the creationism of religion would be true in the realm of the inner/super self (soul, spirit, true self) of man. It is further true that the Creator God, the Moogeuk created all things, maintains, and continues his creation.

(11) The *Ha Do* (河圖) Map, the Yellow River Map was shown to *Bok Hui* (伏羲, Fu Hsi) with a dragon horse with the map of the *Ha Do* (河圖) on its back coming out of the Yellow River. The *Lak Seo* (洛書, the Writing from the River Lo was shown to King Woo (禹, Yu) with a divine turtle with a writing of the *Lak Seo* (洛書) on its back rising from the River Lo.

(12) The *Bok Hui* (伏羲) Eight Trigrams represents the *Ha Do* (河圖) Map and the eight trigrams of birth. It symbolizes the heaven earlier to the earlier heaven of the *Mun Wang* (文王) Eight Trigrams.

(13) The *Mun Wang* (文王) Eight Trigrams is born and represents the eight trigrams of growth of the earlier heaven.

(14) The *Jeong Yeok* (正易) Eight Trigrams is born and represents the eight trigrams of maturity and completion of the later heaven.

(15) Confucius said in *the I Ching* – "Silent fulfillment, confidence that needs no words, depends upon virtuous conducts [7, 8, and 21].

(16) The Analects [7, 8, and 21].

(17) Sum of numbers of positions of *ki* (己) and *moo* (戊), Great Yang (sun) and Geat Yin (moon) is 159= 61+32+36+30. Figure 2 shows four corners of the square in the middle inside the outer ring that indicate the four *sang* (象) of the solar system.

(18) The first hymn singing the metal fire *Jeong Yeok* (金火正易).

(19) *Roe poong* (雷風), thunder wind means the *Jeong Yeok* (正易) Eight Trigrams.

(20) The Ultimate Emperor (皇極) reaches the Non-Ultimate (无極), so it can not be named.

(21) *Yool ryo* (律 呂) sounds seem to imply sounds of movements of sun, moon and Earth, sounds of heaven and earth.

(22) A song that sings the *Jeong Yeok* (正易) Eight Trigrams.

(23) 1 and 6 in north and 3 and 8 in east keep their positions in the *Ha Do* (河圖). North and east are the yang region.

(24) 4 and 9 of south in the *Lak Seo* (洛書) move to west in the *Ha Do* (河圖). 2 and 7 of west in the *Lak* Seo (洛書) move to south in the *Ha Do* (河圖).

(25) The third hymn singing *the Jeong Yeok* (正易).

(26) This describes *kon* (坤) in south in the *Jeong Yeok* (正易) Eight Trigrams.

(27) The Creater God becomes the owner of the gate of metal fire and opens it.

(28) 1 of north in the *Ha Do* moves to left toward southeast; 6 remains in northwest; 3 of east in the *Ha Do* moves to right toward west; 8 remains in east in the *Jeong Yeok* 正 易 Eight Trigrams. See Note (6).

(29) The song of the *Chilwol* (七月) is said to be the product of the Duke of Chou (周公) [8].

(30) Emptiness is position of the *Moogeuk* (无極), the Non-Ultimate. It seems to the author that position of emptiness means omnipresent, everywhere, and 'non-local (David Bohm).

(31) The first day of month is *moo jeen* (无辰) in the earlier heaven.

(32) The former 15 days of a month are the earlier heaven.

(33) The 16th day of month in the later heaven is *moo sool* 戊辰) . The latter 15 days of a month are the later heaven

(34) In the *Lak Seo* (洛書) that represents the earlier heaven, 2, 4, 6 and 8 are at the corner positions; 1, 3, 7 and 9 are in the middle

positions of north, east, west and south, suggesting disharmony and inequality.

(35) In the *Ha Do* (河圖) that represents the later heaven, 1 and 6, 2 and 7, 3 and 8, 4 and 9, and 5 and 10 are in the middle positions in a pair in north, south, east , west, and center, respectively, suggesting harmony and equality.

(36) 6 *Jin* (震) and 1 *Sohn* (巽) in the *Jeong Yeok* (正易) Eight Trigrams.

(37) *Hwa* (化) seems to mean changing and becoming; *Moo* (无), nothingness; *Sangjae* (上帝), the Supreme Emperor, the Creator God.

(38) The moon reaches the straight opposite side of the sun relative to the earth.

(39) The parent is God.

(40) Heaven/earth *bi* (否), standstill represents the earlier heaven.

(41) Earth/Heaven *Tae* (泰), peace represents the later heaven.

(42) *Myo* (卯) of the later heaven becomes the first month of the later heaven. *Yin* (寅) of the first month of the earlier heaven retreats and becomes the twelveth month in the later heaven.

(43) No position seems to correspond to non-locality of wholeness, the totality of David Bohm.

(44) The original heaven fire is understood as source of virtual energy stored in space.

(45) Figure 1 illustrates the 28 *Soo* (宿), Lodges and corresponding western reference stars in the middle and the outer circular bands, respectively. They show location of the sun throughout a year and also at winter (12/22) and summer solstices (6/21), and vernal (3/21) and autumnal (9/23) equinoxes. The inner circular band of the twelve *chi* 支, branch indicates location of the sun in each of twelve months of year. Rotation of the earth, revolution of the moon around the earth, and revolution of the Earth together with

the moon around the sun are counterclockwise and indicated by arrows. Figure 1 illustrates positions of the Earth and the moon on a first day *kye mi* 癸 未 of a first month *myo,* that is a New Year's Day of every year (in the later heaven).

(46) Stomach implies the Lodge *Wi* (胃), Stomach of the 28 *Soo* (宿), Lodges.

(47) Mind implies the Lodge *Sim* (心), Mind of the 28 *Soo* (宿), Lodges.

(48) 55 represents the *Ha Do* (河圖) and 45 the *Lak Seo* 洛書).

(49) A leap month is intercalated in 30 ± months between 2 and 3 years in the lunar calendar.

(50) 1 'sun-year' of the sun to complete one revolution around the galaxy is 24 ten million years. 1 hwa 化 may be possibly 1 ten thousandth of 1 "sun-year", that is, 24,000 years.

(51) Map means the Diagram of Metal Fire *Jeong Yeok Do* (金火正易圖).

(52) Figure 2 of Diagram of Metal Fire *Jeong Yeok Do*(金火正易圖) is composed of the outer ring and the inner square. It seems to me that the outer ring symbolizes heaven, the star-containing universe. The inner square symbolizes the solar system composed of the sun, moon and Earth (as well as planets). Figure 2 seems comparable to Figure 1 of Star Chart. The outer ring of Figure 2 is divided into 24 divisions, corresponding to 12 months and 24 chyul (節) of a year. If the eight trigrams of the *Jeong Yeok* (正易) and four *kan* (干), stem : *kap, eul, kyung,* and *sin* (甲乙庚辛) are properly inserted in the inner circular band of the twelve *chi* (支) of Figure 1, the outer ring of Figure 2 can be obtained that is onsequently assumed to represent heaven, sky, the star-containing universe. Both of Figures 1 and 2 envelope the *Jeong Yeok* (正易) Eight Trigrams. Both Figures 1 and 2 subsequently include the *Ha*

Do because 1, 6 *hae ja* (亥子) in north; 2, 7 *sa oh* (巳午) in south; 4, 9 *shin yoo* (申酉) in west; 3, 8 *yin myo* (寅卯) in east; and 5, 10 *moo ki,* (戊 己) in the center (the solar system in the middle of Figure 1 and the square representing the solar system in Figure 2) are noticed, suggesting a remarkable match between the two diagrams.

The square of Figure 2 has 1, 6 *yim kye* (壬癸) water in north, seemingly corresponding to seas, rivers, lakes, clouds and artesian water around and in the earth, and getting the moon's gravitational force with tide; 2, 7 *byung jeong* (丙丁) fire in south, corresponding to solar energy pouring to the earth and molten rock within the Earth.

Ki 己 in the square is created by union of the *Moogeuk* (无極), the Non-Ultimater 10 and the *Taegeuk* (太極), the Great Ultimate 1. *Ki* 己 is indicated by sum of 10 (+) plus 1 (-), (±) and represents the earth (±). The Moogeuk and the Taegeuk are 10 and 1, being oneness. See note (9).

Moo (戊) 5 symbolizes man, supreme man. The center of the square that is also the center of the outer ring in Figure 2 is empty, indicating the *Moogeuk* 无極, the Creator God who is immanent and transcendent. See notes (56) and (57).

(53) In *chook* (丑) *woon* (運), movement, the moon is in the latter half, 16th to 30th days of month. In *ja* (子) *woon* (運), movement, the moon is in the former half, 1st to 15th days of month.

(54) In the earlier heaven, at midnight of winter solstice, the "winter extreme" in a lunar eleventh month of *kap* (甲) and *ki* (己) year, *kap ja* (甲子) month is born and the third month of the new year is *byung yin* (丙寅). At the same time on *kap* (甲) and *ki* (己) day, *ja* (子) *shi* (時) starts as the beginning of day.

(55) In the later heaven at midnight in a tenth month, (a month *hae* 亥 preceeding to a lunar eleventh month of earlier heaven's winter

solstice) of *ki* 己 and *kap* (甲) year, *kye hae* (癸亥) month is born and the fifth month of the new year is *jeong myo* (丁 卯); at the same time on *ki* (己) and *kap* (甲) day, *hae* (亥) *shi* (時) starts as the beginning of day.

(56) In Figure 2 the center of a square made by *yoo* (酉) 4 metal, *ja* (子) 1 water, *myo* (卯) 8 wood, and oh (午) 7 fire in the circular band is empty, representing the *Moogeuk* (无極), the Non-Ultimate. See note (52).

(57) In Figure 2 the center of a square made by *sa* (巳) 2 fire, *yin* (寅) 3 wood, *hae* (亥) 6 water, and shin (申) 9 metal in the circular band is empty, representing the *Hwanggeuk* (皇極), the Ultmate Emperor.See note (52). Both centers of *Moogeuk* (note 56) and *Hwanggeuk* are one same empty position in the Diagram of Metal Fire *Jeong Yeok Do*, indicating that the *Moogeuk* 无極 and the *Hwanggeuk* (皇極) are oneness and the center of the universe. When a man (man or woman) is spiritually enlightened, he becomes a sage and unites with God.

(58) 3 means the *Bok Hui* (伏羲), the *Mun Wang* (文王) and the *Jeong Yeok* (正易) Eight Trigrams.

(59) The *Bok Hui* (伏羲) Eight Trigrams.

(60) The *Mun Wang* (文王) Eight Trigrams.

(61) The *Jeong Yeok* (正易) Eight Trigrams.

(62) This means that metal fire change opens the later heaven of *the Jeong Yeok* (正易).

(63) In 1885 at the age of 60 years.

(64) In 1881 at the age of 56 years. This year, Kim Hang drew the *Jeong Yeok* (正易) Eight Trigrams.

EPILOGUE

The new quantum theories in modern physics proposed by David Bohm, a great physicist, is based on particle-like and wave-like dual properties of elementary particles such as electrons and photons, proven by Richard Feynman, Nobel Laureate, and their timeless and non-local behavior and movements in which the Einstein's relativity theory and the speed limit of light do not apply.

Richard Feynman said: "Nobody understands quantum mechanics." David Bohm said: "The law of flowing movement of wholeness, the totality that is the deeper foundation of quanta is unknown (probably unknowable)." It seems to me that these statements mean no scientists indeed understand the wholeness and its law of holographic flowing movement without borders, the world beyond the knowable quantum realm at the present time of the contemporary 21st century.

The laws described in *the Jeong Yeok* (正易) seem to me to probably represent super science of new higher order, seemingly the law of wholeness that David Bohm referred to. The terms used in *the Jeong Yeok* seem to be a priori and difficult to comprehend for ordinary people. *Yeok* (易) is so comprehensive and variable and indeed indefinable. It means "change", a calendar, process of change, movement of the sun, moon and Earth, law of creation, and probably plan of God. As Confucius said in his commentaries to *the I Ching* (the Appendix III, Section I, Chapter IX): "The Master said: Whoever knows the *tao* (道), way of the changes and transformations, knows the action of the gods." Words, terms and statements in *the Jeong Yeok* appear to suggest "information" used by David Bohm. Those words, letters, statements like "information" of Bohm seem to be inherently powerful, persistent, creative, existing, evolving and most-likely representing the law of wholeness and foundation of the universe.

I would like to suggest that readers of this book desirably have open mind and/or empty mind in order to see or imagine the world of wholeness that probably reflects its shadow to our physical world of reality. Though I have studied *the Jeong Yeok* in my whole life, the real meaning of *the Jeong Yeok* is quite unknowable to me. At least we, ordinary people may possibly interpret, vaguely understand by applying our modern science and physics to the statements described in *the Jeong Yeok* though they are beyond our comprehension as I mentioned in the chapters 11 and 12 of the author's book *Seeking a New World* [6].

It seems to me, to my knowledge, that there is no translation in English of the original *Jeong Yeok* (正易) published in Korea although it was partly introduced to the western world by Jung Young Lee [10] and me [5]. I feel that it is time for me to translate in English the original *Jeong Yeok* (正易)written in Chinese characters on the basis of my learning, hearing, reading and reasoning regarding *the Jeong Yeok* throughout my life in order to help others who want to know and/or study *the Jeong Yeok*. The late Dr. Jeong Ho Yi, one of the outstanding scholars of *the Jeong Yeok* and *the I Ching* in Korea, asked me in his letter to contribute to globalization of *the Jeong Yeok*.

I would like to recommend that readers to read the Lee's book "*The Theory of Change*" and his article "*The origin and significance of the*

Chongyok or Book of Correct Change" as well as my book, *Seeking a New World* [6] in order to study *the Jeong Yeok* and *the I Ching*.

I would take full responsibility for any errors in my translation of *the Jeong Yeok* that I may have made. I humbly pray the errors would be corrected in future.

REFERENCES

1. Bailey, Alice A. *The Reappearance of the Christ.* Lucis Publishing Co., New York, 2006.
2. _____. *The Consciousness of the Atom.* Lucis Publishing Co., New Lucis Publishing Co., New York, 1981 (83).
3. Bohm, David. *Wholeness and the Implicate Order.* Routledge, New York, 2006.
4. Chung, Bongkil. *The Scriptures of Won Buddhism.* University of Hawai'i Press, Honolulu, 2005 (12-8, 342).
5. Cull, Christopher. *Astronomy and Mathematics in Ancient China: Zhou bi jing.* Cambridge University Press, Cambridge, UK, 1996 (17-8)
6. Chung, Sung J. *Seeking a New World.* iUniverse, Bloomington, Indiana, 2009.
7. Chung, Tsai Chih. *Confucius Speaks.* Doubleday, New York, 1996 (61, 128)
8. Kim, Hang, 정역 正易, *Jeong Yeok.* The original Chinese Text Print with the text translated in Korean by Jeong Ho Yi. The Asian Culture Press, Seoul, Korea, 1990 (3, 8, 19, 60, 61, 76, 78, 80, 106-7, 121).

9. Knitter, F. Paul. *Without Buddha I Could Not Be a Christian.* Oneworld, Oxford, 2009 (112-7, 129, 216).

10. Lee, Jung Young. *The Theory of Change.* Orbis Books, New York, 1979.

11. _____. The origin and significance of the Chongyok or Book of Changes. *Journal of Chinese Philosophy* 9 (1982) 211-41.

12. Legge, James. Translated. *The I Ching.* Dova Publications, New York, 1963 (1, 366, 369, 427).

13. Lowenstein, Tom. *Buddhist Inspirations.* Duncan Bairs Publishers, London, 2005 (65).

14. Meddegama, Udaya. Translated. *Anagatavamsa Desana: The Chronicle-To-Be.* Edited with an Introduction, Glossary and Notes by John Clifford Holt. Motilal Banarsidass Publishers, Dehli, India, 1993.

15. Nichol, Lee. *The Essential David Bohm.* Routledge, New York, 2006.

16. Rey, H. A. *The Stars.* Houghton Mufflin Company, Boston, Massachusetts, 1980 (118, 134).

17. Rinpoche, Sogyal. *The Tibetan Book of Living and Dying.* Harper SanFrancisco, New York, 1993 (270).

18. Ross, Frank, Jr. *Oracles, Bones, Stones and Wheelbarrows: Ancient Chinese Science and Technology.* Houghton Muffin Company, Boston, Massachusetts, 1982 (14-8).

19. Sach, Jacky. *Everything Buddhism Book.* Adams Media Corporation, Avon, Massachusetts, 2003 (27, 122, 171).

20. Sardar, Ziauddin. *What Do Muslims Believe? The Roots and Realities of Modern Islam.* Walker Publishing Co., New York, 2007 (61, 75, 113, 115).

21. Wilhelm, Richard. The I Ching or *Book of Changes* (translated). Rendered into English by Cary F. Baynes. Rutledge & Kegan Paul, London, 1967 (272, 309, 311, 329)

22. Yi, Jeong Ho. Concernig the Jeong Yeok. *Korean Religion 7* (1982) 5-25.

23. _____. *Jeong Yeok Yeonggoo* (text in Korean). The Gookjae University Press, Seoul, Korea, 1976 (60, 85, 203, 215, 224, 286).

24. _____. *The I Ching Jeongeui* (text in Korean). The Asian Culture Press, Seoul, Korea, 1980 (71, 175).

25. _____. *The Third Yeok Hak* (text in Korean). The Asian Culture Press, Seoul, Korea, 1992 (62, 150).

26. Yogananda, Pramahansa. *To Be Victorious in Life.* Self-Realization Fellowship, Los Angeles, California, 2002 (10).

27. Yum, Dong Ho. "Rest, play. Do not work "is a motto of a company (text in Korean). *Monthly Chosun* (2009) (month 10) 528-38.